STOP SELLING REAL ESTATE & START HELPING PEOPLE

Matilda Nestoroska

◻INDENT
PUBLISHING
IndentPublishing.com

Stop Selling Real Estate
& Start Helping People

Print edition first published in Canada in 2024
ebook edition published 2024

Cover design by Deena Hasan Rizwan
Cover photography: Agnes Kiesz/Pure Studios

Indent Publishing
indentpublishing.com
contact@indentpublishing.com

Nestoroska, Matilda
Stop Selling Real Estate & Start Helping People

ISBN 978-1-998904-11-2

TABLE OF CONTENTS

TABLE OF CONTENTS

INTRODUCTION

Every new startup business is an ESS! (That's not a typo ☺). It is Exciting, Scary and Stressful too.

You have an idea to become a realtor ®, you THINK you know everything there is to know (hey, how hard can it be to sell houses? You show it to a buyer, and you sell it, right?) and then you get a rude awakening. From a smooth run, it becomes a hurdle marathon. Challenge after challenge after challenge. Once you realize that you need to run a business and not just become a "realtor," you go "uh-oh." If you had a business before – I should have said a successful business before – you will be just fine, but if you were a full-time employee for most of your career and you don't know how to run a business, you'll be in deep "doo-doo."

You are smart, so you'll start asking questions, you'll start reading different books (like this one) to help you establish your business and to grow it, you'll visit seminars – and the list goes on.

When I got my licence here in Ontario, I thought it would be a great idea for me to read some experts books, to understand better how real estate here in Canada works, since I had experience in real estate only in Europe. I've tried to find some books with tips how not to screw up. There are many motivational books out there, there are many business books, there are many books with "real estate" in the title, but very few actually had some real "hands-on" tips and ideas for someone who is just starting a new business and does not know much about it.

So, I had to learn as a I go. I've implemented what I could from my previous experience, but that was not enough. Through the years in business, I had some smaller hiccups, but I surely learned from them and never repeated the same ones again. I've dealt with many new and experienced agents who were making some small and not so small crucial mistakes. Some of them were on such "simple" tasks too. So, I learned from them too.

I've seen people quitting real estate by saying how the job is not good, how it is hard, lonely, and how they didn't know what to do, and even worse, they think they did it all right, but not sure how come they didn't succeed.

That is the reason why I am writing this book: to help all of you real estate "rookies" out there to have a better start to achieve your results sooner, rather than later, and hopefully with much less pain. This is supposed to be a road map for you, with real tips and tricks of what to do, and what not to do. It is all explained in a very simple language, so everyone can understand it from reading it the first time. No 25-letter words that only someone with a PhD can understand, no philosophical BS, so it can look like I am "extra" smart. Just simple ideas and advice.

Most of the information and tips I will provide you, as an agent with close to two decades of experience on two continents, you might know and yet never have used. However, I am sure you will find at least one thing you can implement, or improve, in your business that will result in bringing you some extra revenue, more free time and fewer "ulcer attacks." If you pick up at least one idea that results in you getting one deal, it will be a worthwhile business expense and the time spent reading this book will have been a wise decision.

Let me clarify one thing: I am not reinventing the wheel in this book. This is simply a book of compiled information, instructions and hard-earned lessons from my personal and painful experience, and some of my colleagues' experience too. This book will provide you with a list of tasks and tools that have helped me and many other realtors to achieve their goals and become reputable and successful real estate professionals in our industry. I've spent years collecting information through trial and error, from my personal experience in Europe, Canada and, lately, with help from some dear colleagues in the U.S. too. I kept what worked and discarded what didn't. I listened to my colleagues about what worked for them and where they failed too and made sure to write those down as well. This way, I hope to save you a few years of your own failures and headaches. I will share the mistakes with you, so you can learn from them. And don't worry, I am sure there are still plenty of mistakes of your own that you will make through the years to come.

We all know that people learn best from their own mistakes, but those also hurt the most. Why repeat what everyone else does and go through all that pain and expense when you can be smarter and learn from someone else's mistakes?

Now, before you do any of that, you should dissect your current lifestyle. Are you are ready for a new life journey?

CHAPTER 1

WHY IN THE WORLD
DID I DO THIS?

How many times have you thought, or screamed out loud, "why in the world do I do this?"

You go to school, finish it – or not, it doesn't matter. Life takes its course and you start working. It is kind of expected for you to finish school (or not), find a job, get married (or not), have children (or not), have pets (or not), wait to retire (or not) and eventually die (or not).

Wait. Sorry, you WILL die ☺

That is the one and only absolute truth in this universe. Death and paying taxes will catch up with you eventually. Everything else is debatable. Now, if we are all sure we will die, we just don't know when, why live a life filled with fear? And, most importantly, why live a life you hate?

How many times per day do you see people sharing posts about how they hate their jobs, hate Mondays, love TGIF, hate 9 a.m. but love 5 p.m.? And all the rest.

Some people keep saying how much they hate their jobs, their bosses, their colleagues. And yet they continue working the same job for many years, even decades. Why?

Many years ago, a friend of mine went into this kind of spiraling. After constant nagging, almost every time we met, I'd ask: "So, if you hate your job that much, how come you don't change what you do to something you will actually enjoy doing?" She'd reply: "What? That means I would need to go back to school and take the risk of not finding a job for some time!" To which I said: "OK, to recap: You hate your life, you don't want to change anything in it and you don't want to risk anything? So, what will you do? Continue complaining for the rest of your life?"

A few years later, she finished some other school, then another one, then another one, and I think she got "the drift" and took action. So, enjoy life to the fullest and don't "settle." I know it sounds corny, but you DO have only one life to live, so why waste it?

Why did I share this story? For you to clarify your own life, if you are in similar shoes. And I say it as a someone who means you well, I rode that rollercoaster ride too.

If you are in a similar situation, and that is a reason you have picked up this book to read, then I congratulate you on taking action and for being a "doer" not a "whiner." (Yeah, this book is about being informative, yet blunt. I am not here to give you a shoulder to cry on, but rather give you the tools to become successful. And to stop crying along the way, hopefully ☺)

On the other hand, if you are in the real estate business already and just want to see if there is anything to help you achieve better results, then this book is for you too, regardless of how long you have been in the business.

When I visit any seminar, read any book, or go for a coaching session, my ultimate goal is to pick up one idea, and one idea only! I used to write all the awesome ideas I hear about, and then I'd completely forget about them, because once I see the list, it becomes too overwhelming. I would put the booklet and my notes in the TOP drawer of my desk (to remind me how important it is), and once I closed that drawer, I closed my mind to it too.

Once I started selecting only one idea to implement immediately, I actually did it! So, learn from my mistake: You can write all good ideas, but circle ONLY one that you will implement as soon as you can. The rest of them you can write down in an order in which you will implement them. That way you actually might implement them.

You're welcome!

CHAPTER 2

ROAD MAP TO STARTING YOUR REAL ESTATE BUSINESS

Is the real estate profession the next chapter in your fun and happy life's journey? In this chapter we will try to figure that one out.

Real estate might be for you, and it might not be, but I sincerely hope this book will help you clear your vision, regardless of which direction you will take.

Now, let's get to work, dig deep and dissect all the pros and cons of real estate and see if it matches your expectations.

What is it that you REALLY want from the real estate profession, so you can avoid years of heartaches, unnecessary stress and expenses too?

ASK YOURSELF:

1. Am I cut out to be a realtor?
2. Is there a difference among brokerages and how do I choose one that fits me the best?
3. What is my desired yearly income and do I have a business plan on how to achieve it? (Be realistic.)
4. Can I maintain a similar lifestyle until the income from real estate transactions comes? (It might take three to six months before you see a penny,

and that is only if you are REALLY good and have maybe a great mentor and/or your office and real estate boards provide good training.)

5. Am I responsible enough to keep myself on track?
6. Do I have my family's support?
7. Will this career change pay the same, less, or more money?

Before we start analyzing each question, let me clear up one thing for you first:

Would it be OK to change your career, regardless of the answers above?

My answer is: Absolutely YES!

You might not get more money quickly (unless you are looking for an immediately better-paying job), but with persistence and not "hating" your job, you will eventually hit the mark you were dreaming about. And then hopefully you will surpass it, and you will make it double or triple… The bonus is that you will achieve that goal while having peace and happiness too (well, most of the time … until you meet and close that client who pisses you off to the moon and back … repeatedly).

You will wake up every morning with a purpose and will cope with challenges easier than if you were waking up every morning and dragging your feet to a job you absolutely hate. That is a mental and physical drain that no one should be living for years in and out.

I remember on one of the first trainings I had in the office. We were told to put a number we hoped to make that year and then to increase it by 25 per cent every year after that. We were supposed to look at year 5 in the business. That number scared the cr@# out of me but guess what?! I reached that number by year 3 and not 5! Where there is a will, there is a way. You will hear me repeating this a few more times in this book. I sincerely believe in it, and I hope it can become your mantra too.

Going back to real estate: If you already have a real estate licence, what is your "why"? Why did you join real estate?

If you tell me, "so I can make a sh@# load of money in 30 days or less," I strongly advise you to put this book down and go back to your old job.

When we came to Canada, a few decades ago, I tried different careers, before I had my "AHA" moment.

I worked the same way, every day, regardless of the type of the job I had. And I DID like the jobs themselves. However, I simply hated being "restrained" in the cubicle, every day from 9 a.m. to 5 p.m.

The breaking point was missing my young son growing up. Every time he would get sick, I had to beg to leave work and take him to the doctor's office. One day, coming back from yet another doctor's appointment, I asked myself. "Why in the world am I doing this to myself?? I left my child with a fever this morning, to go to work? I love my husband, but he is not ME! No one can take better care of my child than I can! (I know, I am a control freak and a "helicopter parent," but screw it. I love my kids more than my life!)

Back to my epiphany. I asked myself: If I don't like this,

what DO I like? I Love helping people, I love working when I want, and how I want, I love to be appreciated and above all I love spending time with my family.

I remembered when I had my real estate brokerage in Europe how much I liked my freedom. Being a business owner was stressful, of course, but I enjoyed helping people get their new homes. I felt appreciated (most of the time) once the whole real estate transaction was done. I loved being able to make my own rules and hours, loved not having a boss, no colleagues to piss me off. Just me, myself and I. When I screwed up, there was no one to blame but me, and when I won, no one would take credit for it but me.

"I am my own boss; I create my own destiny and I adore spending time with my family. The success will follow." THAT was my turning point.

Don't worry about the "how." That will come slowly, but surely, if you have your clear "why." The "how" can be learned. You just need to be patient, willing to listen and actually DO the work you are supposed to do.

Let's break those questions down now:

1. AM I CUT OUT TO BE A REALTOR?

To be great at the real estate profession, you should like working with people, the selling should be in your blood and you should be very much interested in negotiating.

Sales techniques and negotiation can be learned and improved. But if you are NOT a "people-y person," then you will have a bit of a rockier road ahead of you. You can still achieve great success, but it will take more energy, and it might take a bit more time too. What do I mean by that?

You've probably heard people say, "I am an introvert" or "I am an extrovert and I love it!" If you don't know what those words mean, feel free to Google the proper "fancy" definitions of them. In the meantime, I will explain them to you in plain English.

Introvert – People, don't talk to me!
Extrovert – Talking to people is my superpower!

You MUST figure out which one you are before you do anything in real estate – and I mean anything! Forget prospecting or showings! You need to figure out who you are, what would you need to do, to adjust to this new business role requirements, and that will lead you to the most successful way of doing the business your way – which will bring you happiness and money, of course.

Let me give you some examples of how your personality can directly affect the way you will do real estate. If you are introverted, doing door knocking will be excruciating for you. Just the thought of meeting strangers and trying to sell them your real estate services will likely give you anxiety, so this way of doing business might not be right for you.

Open houses might be a tough cookie for you too, and I'm not even going to talk about hosting a micro-, or a large-scale event. Being surrounded by a large number of people might block you from thinking straight. However, with some training and with experience, you might become more used to people, and who knows, you might even start enjoying being surrounded by people. Just kidding! That's not likely to happen, but you will hopefully learn to "tolerate" people better.

How about being claustrophobic? Can that cause you some pain in this business? Absolutely! You will need to have a plan "B" in case you have a severe case of it. Maybe have a fellow agent show those properties to your clients.

I was very claustrophobic. Confined spaces were making my heart beat so hard that I could feel my heart in my throat. My ears would start ringing and I couldn't breathe. It was like someone was choking me. I started my career with first-time homebuyers who could mostly afford condominium apartments (lucky me ☺). Going into elevators, sometimes all the way to the 40th floor, or higher, were horrifying experiences for me. It took lot of my strength not to show to my clients how scared I am of the elevators. Remember, I have a huge ego and wouldn't show anyone that I have any kind of weaknesses (what a dumba@# was I ?!)

Once I was locked out in the stairway where the realtors kept the lockboxes. I was banging on the door like crazy until my client heard me at the end of the hallway. Since then, I always block the door with my purse, regardless of if the door has the auto-lock on it or not. Another time, I was showing a "one and a half storey" house in Hamilton, and as we started going upstairs, suddenly the ceiling was literally above my head. The room started spinning and I just excused myself and told clients I will wait for them downstairs. Not a fun experience. It took me years of learning how to control this fear, and by being exposed to this challenge daily, for so long, it actually helped me so much that I even managed to go on a cruise ship (a room with a balcony though, I'm not THAT much healed ☺). So, again, when there is a will, there is a way (or you just need to be a nut-job like me ☺)

Let's go back to agents who are introverts and what could be their source of income.

Social media, lead-generating systems and farming might be good for you.

With some good mentoring and lots of practice – and by practice I mean KEEP PROSPECTING – you should be able to get out of your comfort zone and should be able to host great open houses (maybe team up with a fellow realtor) and even host large events.

You will definitely feel drained after those tasks, but that should be your "drive," to make as many leads as possible during those events and open houses, so your "suffering" was worth it. (Something like me being claustrophobic but I kept showing condominiums anyway ☺)

If you are an extrovert, door knocking shouldn't be a problem and hosting open houses and events might be just right for you. That could potentially be your main source of income too.

Social media might be a bit "boring" for you, so maybe it's best to outsource that one, if you can afford it. If you have teenage kids, they can be your "cheap" labour too. They can do it for you and definitely better than you, until you start having positive cashflow. Then you can outsource it to the professionals.

You can use that extra time to prospect, in a way that suits you and will bring the results too.

What an efficient way of being productive and happy, don't you agree?

The level of your success and how fast you will get there will depend on you and your determination to succeed.

As I've heard so many times before, the real estate profession is simple, but NOT easy!

When I first joined a real estate brokerage here in Canada, I went for a monthly office meeting. The broker of record, Nelson Goulart (amazing guy BTW), introduced me to some fellow agents. One of them started talking to me about how "real estate is a tough business" and how it is "not good," that she had been in the business for six months and she still hadn't made a single deal. I remember feeling a bit uncomfortable and thinking, What the heck did I get myself into?

Just to go back in time a bit: A few years before we immigrated to Canada, we had our own real estate brokerage in Europe, and I knew how real estate sales work. The biggest difference is that we didn't have mortgages there. All transactions were done in cash. Ah, the good old "briefcase" times.

Now, back to that meeting: The meeting was over and I decided to focus really hard on my business, since, according to that lady, it was a "very tough business" here. Six months later, I'd already made a few deals. I even got a listing, which is not that common for a "newbie."

I was going regularly to our monthly meetings, since we always had great speakers coming in. At one of the meetings, approximately six months later, as I was passing by, I overheard the same lady saying to a new agent: "Oh, this business is very hard. I wish I hadn't got into it. It's been a whole year and I still haven't made a single deal." The lightbulb went on in my head. It is not the real estate business that is the problem, I thought. It is you and your attitude.

Complaining will not get you anywhere. Learning and being able to listen will get you far. And so will being willing to implement what works.

2. IS THERE A DIFFERENCE AMONG BROKERAGES AND HOW DO I CHOOSE ONE THAT FITS ME THE BEST?

We've figured out if you are an introvert or an extrovert (not that you didn't know that already) and hopefully you have determined what will be your main focus for generating leads: open houses, events, cold calls, door knocking, farming etc. (We will speak in depth about these prospecting options later in the book.)

Try not to think of how many buyers' and sellers' leads you have now. If you are a new or newer agent, very likely you have zero to none. And that's OK! It is a good sign that at least you DO know how many leads you don't have yet. You will learn later in the book how to find those leads, though, so keep going. I mean reading.

If it is your first year in real estate, with some great training and/or mentoring, you should be able to make a deal within the first three to six months. Therefore, you should be joining a brokerage based on the training and support they provide.

We have to determine which brokerage to join. How do you determine which one is the best for you?

There are too many brokerages out there to choose from. There are some that most have heard of and are known all over the world. "Big Franchise" brokerages.

Then, there are some that are known as "discount" brokerages, there are some "luxury homes" brokerages and there are some "boutique brokerages" too. I am sure there are many other different brokerage types, but for now, as a beginner, these are more than enough for you to choose from.

"BIG FRANCHISE" BROKERAGES

Big franchise brokerages have determined what is the percentage they want to receive from you and the only difference between different big franchises is how they will split the cost. That is, lower commission split plus monthly fee, or higher commission split and no/low monthly fee, etc. They are usually well known among the public and I was lucky enough to be a part of a company like that, for a very long time. Truly amazing people at RE/MAX Aboutowne Realty in Oakville. All the way from the owner of the franchise to the management team, supporting team and front desk team too. It is a very good environment to be in. But not all the franchises are the same, so pay more attention to all these departments before you commit to one. Here are some pros and cons of these type of brokerages:

PROS:
These brokerages usually provide good training, full-time personnel to help with listing uploading, offers preparation, "high traffic" websites offering some leads, "in-house" marketing departments, mortgage specialists and lawyers, great offices with free meeting

rooms, plenty of industry training, motivational speakers and more. They're a good option for experienced agents who are looking to expand and to target the "brand-loving" clients, and good even for "newbie" agents with a stronger financial budget.

CONS:

The monthly/annual fee is on the higher end. Besides a regular commission split, there will likely be monthly fees extra, regardless of if you made a deal or not. This might be a difficult choice for someone who is just starting and doesn't have funds available for a new business, but can be a great motivator for you to work more, so you can have a profit after all expenses.

"NO FRILLS" BROKERAGES

Some brokerages known as "discount" brokerages will charge only a small fee per deal, but then the level of the service provided might be completely different from what most of the big franchises or boutique brokerages offer.

I am sure there are some discount brokerages that have great agents and managers who will try to help as much as they can. Having limited funds coming in from the agents' fees, it is not expected for them to hire big speakers and live trainings for free.

PROS:

Ultra-low commission fee and monthly expense.

Some brokerages will offer nice office space and meeting rooms too. Some will have in-house mortgage specialists and some form of online training. This setup might be a good option for seasoned agents who do not need any big support from the office and are just "expense wise."

CONS:

There might be some support, but not much. Free, in-person training is likely very limited, if it exists at all. You are responsible for your listings uploads and offer preparation, and making sure that they are all accurate and following the board association rules. If you are just beginning in the real estate business, you need all the help you can get, and shouldn't rely solely on what you've learned in the licensing phase, which is equivalent to zero. So, think twice before you decide to choose this kind of brokerage. If you do, please make sure you have a great coach/mentor, and/or team up with a seasoned realtor and learn as much as you can, since you will need lots of help if you are planning to survive and succeed in this business.

"NOT-SO-FAMOUS" BROKERAGES

Some smaller franchises and brokerages might not be well known in your local area, and that might make you think that you shouldn't be joining them, because "people will not recognize them." However, what you need to do is to research them well. Check the level of support they provide, how many agents are in the brokerage and how many listings they have on the local boards. Some of them will pleasantly surprise you with the amenities and level of service they provide to their agents, and some will make you feel like a part of their family. I was blessed to belong to one brokerage like that, early in my career, led by an amazing Broker of record Nelson Goulart and his wife Maria Goulart.

PROS:

These brokerages will likely provide a great level of services to agents. There will be in-person training and it's more likely the whole support team will know you by your first name, since they usually don't have very many agents per office. They will have nice offices and meeting rooms too. Some will even have a higher level of service than what the big franchises offer. This type of brokerage I call a "golden middle." There are usually different commission split options, they shouldn't have high extra fees, as big franchise companies do, and could be a good option for new agents with a limited budget.

CONS:

The commission splits are similar to what the big franchises charge, minus the usual hefty monthly/yearly fee. Also, they won't likely have that recognizable "branding" to give you that boost.

However, I strongly believe that this might work to your advantage, and I shouldn't really count it as a "con." If you can compete with the big-name brokerages and still get loyal clients, then you are set for success.

When I first got my licence in Ontario, I joined GMAC Signature Service. That real estate franchise was well known in the United States, but not so much in Ontario, Canada. That didn't stop me becoming a trusted realtor to many clients and quite a few of them became my repeat clients – and lifelong friends too.

A few years into my real estate career in Canada, one of the people I know was debating with me, saying how one can be a successful real estate agent ONLY if they are members of big-franchise real estate brokerages.

I was trying to explain that the buyers and sellers connect with an agent him/herself and not the brand. That agent's knowledge, experience and trustworthiness will land them more clients, and repeated clients too.

So, just to prove to them that even though the brand's name helps, it absolutely is NOT that crucial for getting business and more importantly repeat business, I decided to test that theory.

When two of my repeat clients and now dear friends, Kim

and Gary, called me to discuss another real estate transaction again, I asked: "Hey, guys, which real estate brokerage am I with? To which Gary responded: "I don't know, something with a funny name."

The moral of this story: People will work with YOU, if they like you, know you and trust you, and not because you are affiliated with a big company. Well, at least most people.

Act in the best possible interest of your client and success will follow. Don't live or expect to live on someone else's glory.

That brand name might get your foot in the door, but if you are not working in your clients' best interest, if you don't show them that you truly care and obey your fiduciary duties towards them, they will lose trust in you, and you will lose their business.

Now that we've learned more about different types of brokerages, let's have some fun with "plain English" examples, to help you with selecting a brokerage that will fit you, your budget and your experience level.

Brokerage "X" offers you a 70/30 commission split and they offer a calendar full of in-person training throughout the month. Their office will help you with offers/deals paperwork and so on. They have many listings to share with you, to advertise and/or host open houses. They often have very nice and presentable offices, offer you an in-house marketing department, a mortgage specialist to help you with pre-qualifying clients on the spot. Like the theme song says on that great old TV show *Cheers*, they're somewhere "where everybody knows your name."

As opposed to that, there is a Brokerage "Y" (read "whyyyyyyy?"). They are charging you "only" $XXX per deal and there is likely NO in-person training where you can ask questions. They offer limited support and you have to upload and do your paperwork yourself. (Maybe, just maybe, they might have online tutorials on how to upload the documents.)

So, if you are just starting the business and you are trying to be "expense wise," please DO be wise and calculate what is actually a better choice for you at that stage in your career.

If nobody is there to teach you how to prospect, how to do a listing presentation, how to convince buyers to sign that Buyers Representation Agreement when you meet with them for a buyer's presentation, how to create a business plan, or what a business plan even IS, what should you include in the offer, if the furnace and air conditioning are rentals, what is a form 127 and so much more – then that brokerage is maybe not the right choice for you, at least not at this moment.

BROKERAGE COMPARISON	
Brokerage X SPLIT: 70% - 30%	Brokerage Y FLAT FEE: $XXX / deal
INCOME $100,000	INCOME $0
YOU: $70,000 BROKERAGE: $30,000	YOU: $0 BROKERAGE: $0
Total income: $70,000	Total income: $0

A 70/30, split from $100,000 seems much better than $0 from $0 income.

Right?

Your mindset has to be set straight. You "invest" in your business, not "spend"!

Another reason I see that you should invest in the brokerage with in-person training is if you invest more, it is more likely you will work harder (read "smarter"), so you can cover those expenses and still earn money for the food on your table and that dream vacation.

Let's look it from a different angle:

Some of the great ways of generating new leads (since you have zilch as a new agent) and to grow your database (which is likely tiny) are open houses and listing advertising.

Since you likely won't have a listing as soon as you get your licence, I suggest new agents reach out to more experienced agents in the office and ask for permission to advertise their listings or to host an open house for them.

If the discounting Brokerage "Y" has a very limited number of agents and listings, how will you be able to get that starting point and get some leads? I assume paid lead-generating advertising is not even an option for now.

I'll repeat again: Choose wisely which brokerage you are joining. FYI, you can always change the brokerage. It is not the end of the world.

Full disclosure: I do NOT get anything from promoting any specific types of brokerages. This is merely my observation and my personal opinion. You absolutely do not need to agree with me. Just do the math and go with your gut!

3. WHAT IS MY DESIRED YEARLY INCOME AND DO I HAVE A BUSINESS PLAN ON HOW TO ACHIEVE IT?

You have decided what kind of brokerage to join and my question to you is what is your desired income for your first year in the real estate business? How many deals will you make and which source of income will they come from?

Please stop rolling your eyes and don't call me crazy! I can read your mind right now!

Yes! you MUST have a goal, even if you don't have any clients, leads or even people in your database. If you don't know where you are going on vacation, how can you get ready? Do you take winter clothes, or summer clothes? Do you need snow skis or water skis?

Don't worry, there is logic in this madness, just bear with me for a moment.

These above questions are the bones of any business plan. Regardless of the business. Let me repeat those points:

BUSINESS PLAN FOUNDATIONS:

⊚ DESIRED YEARLY INCOME
⊚ SOURCE OF INCOME
⊚ MARKETING PLAN TO ACHIEVE THE GOAL

A business plan is your road map. Without it, you will be clueless and will go through the business as if you were a tiny mosquito trying to fly during a windstorm.

But if you have one, you will be a smart mosquito who entered a speeding truck and will ride safely through the storm.

We will not go into depth here about business planning, since that is a book, or two, on its own. I will just scratch the surface and talk about the goal-setting calculations you must have if you want to succeed. You can speak with your office manager, coach, mentor, fellow agent and/or hopefully visit those in-person trainings to learn more about creating a strong and achievable business plan. Here is how to determine your yearly goal:

STEP 1:

> Write down how many deals this year you would like or hope to make in your first year. (Be realistic.) Also, your business year doesn't have to be from January to December. It can be June to May or any other 12-month period you choose.

STEP 2:

> Find an average selling price for the area you think you will be working in. You can find it on your local real estate board market statistics page or ask your office manager to help you with it – unless you have the tracked numbers from your deals from a previous year, of course.

STEP 3:

Multiply the number of deals with the average selling price amount and you will get your yearly goal. (see the example below)

Example:
YEARLY INCOME CALCULATION

Goal:
- 6 Deals
- Average Commission $15,000

Deals Breakdown:
- 2 Deals – SOI
- 1 Deal – Open House
- 1 Deal – Door knocking
- 1 Deal – Online Marketing
- 1 Deal – Networking

Total Income: 6 Deals x $15,000 = $90,000

Not bad for a first year, isn't it? Will it be easy to do it? Not really. Can it be done? Absolutely! (If you do the work AND ask for help when needed.)

STEP 4:

Determine what will be your source of income. Choose ones you feel comfortable, or somewhat comfortable to do. If it is only one or two sources, it's OK. Focus on the tasks that you will actually do.

SOURCE OF INCOME EXAMPLES

- sphere of influence (database referral)
- open house

- ☺ door knocking
- ☺ online leads
- ☺ cold calling
- ☺ networking (BNI, Rotary Club, Chamber of Commerce, Community Groups, etc)

So, to wrap up this section, here are some tips for you:

TIP 1:

Speak with your brokerage and ask for help on how to create a business plan and how to be held accountable for executing it. i.e., check-in every week, or every two weeks to review your numbers, your progress and what are the troubles you are experiencing at that moment.

TIP 2:

Attend regular office meetings, so you can meet more senior agents (I mean senior by experience, not age!) They are the ones who you will be asking to advertise their listings and host open houses for them. It will be easier for you to get their blessing once they get to know how awesome you are.

TIP 3:

Go to office trainings (assuming there are some) and make sure you ask questions. Remember, there is no such thing as a "stupid" question. Listen to what other agents are asking and learn, learn, learn.

TIP 4:

Visit seminars organized by mortgage brokers, banks, inspectors, or lawyers to learn the vocabulary and terms and to keep yourself up to date with all current trends, changes and more. Try to go to in-person seminars any time you get a chance. That way you can network and potentially grow your database of trusted services and, who knows, maybe they will become your clients too.

Once you have a business plan in place, you will need to start working on how to actually get those leads, to convert to clients, to convert to deals. I will share some great ideas, steps and tips with you later in this book. For now, I am trying to keep the whole process of becoming a successful realtor all in order, as it should be.

You can't run with a basket to go to pick those apples if you haven't even planted the damn tree yet! So keep reading, be patient (which is usually not a strength of many realtors) and you will thank me later.

4. CAN I MAINTAIN A SIMILAR LIFESTYLE UNTIL THE INCOME FROM REAL ESTATE TRANSACTIONS COMES IN?

One of the biggest contributors toward the real estate professional's failure is that there was no budgeting plan in place.

People very often decide to "try real estate" on impulse. They likely got angry with their current boss or colleague. Or they know of someone in real estate who keeps flashing their fancy car, or posts smiling faces from vacation, without realizing how much work, trial and error and sacrificing was likely in that realtor's business AND PERSONAL life before they actually achieved that "flashiness."

They think, ah, six months of "night school" classes, I get the licence and anybody can sell five or six houses per year" – "easy-peasy."

Boy, are they wrong or what?

My sincere advice to you is to have answers to the questions below, before you tell your current boss to go to hell:

⊚ How much will it cost me to finish the real estate college? (Yeah, yeah, I know you've checked that one already, and that is only for the classes! But, how about the next few questions? Do you have answers to those questions?)

⊚ How long will the school last? (be realistic)

⊚ Will I quit my job before, or after I finish college?

⊚ Which brokerage will I join?

⊚ How much will my monthly expenses be, including board memberships, insurances, brokerage fees, regardless of whether I make any deals or not (there are many brokerages that have monthly fees on top of commission splits)

⊚ Do I have enough money to maintain a similar lifestyle for the next six months to a year, without getting a single deal done?

How is your ulcer or headache now?

If you have answers to all those questions – actually, I should have said, if you have "satisfactory" answers to all those questions – then you are off to a great start, and I can see you succeeding way faster than most of the other realtors out there. If not, well, think fast, since you're already deep into the mud.

I will try to help you a bit with some of those nasty questions. We will focus mostly on the last question in regards to your "safety net," since everything else is straightforward.

If you have a spouse who is employed, maybe they can help a bit. But still, speak with a good accountant and a banker and try to figure out your "safety net" that will be there to protect you if needed. (Don't touch it to buy shoes or a car though, please.) You can meet clients in your family van, or a smaller car too. The buyers and sellers don't care much what car you are driving. They care about how you will help them achieve their goal in the shortest amount of time with the best possible terms.

Now, even though having no deals done in the first six months seems like a pretty bad situation, it has a silver lining to it.

This will be a test on how well you are working under pressure. Also, it should be your motivator, to keep you on top of your tasks, keep you on track and help you achieve the desired results faster.

If you don't do well under the stress, then again you might consider thanking me for the advice and try to look for another job that might not be as bad as your previous one but still has secure and regular paystubs.

To calculate how big your "safety net" should be, please write down all your fixed expenses (mortgage, cars, utility bills, real estate memberships and whatever else), budget for your monthly meal expenses, children's activities if any and a vacation. And leave some extra room for unplanned expenses (car repair, house problems and so on).

After adding all those together, multiply that amount by 12 and that will be the amount you should ideally have in your bank accounts.

You've probably rolled your eyes (again) when you read "vacation." Well, don't. Just because you're starting a new business doesn't mean you need to sacrifice your lifestyle and sanity. Don't make the mistake I did: I was so focused on my business that I forgot to live!

The worst thing you can say is, "I'll work for a few years without vacation and then I will catch up." WRONG! That time will have passed and you will never get it back. DREAM BIG, but don't sacrifice! Instead – adjust.

If you are money-conscious, instead of going for a 10-day luxury cruise, go seven days to the Caribbean. Or, if even that seems too big, go seven days somewhere local. It doesn't matter what it is, it matters that it is called A VACATION, and that you will NOT be working for those seven days. I know, people who know me and read this, are saying now "Matilda, you're full of sh@#! You've been working from all vacations you went to, from different countries, continents and time zones."

As I said before, don't repeat my mistakes. Do better.

We all know that we learn best from our own mistakes, but they hurt the most. Therefore, I am suggesting that you learn from mine and everyone else's mistakes. You can still learn, and it will be less painful.

For many years, I've been going to a Richard Robins International conferences (RichardRobbins.com), and almost every year he would make sure to remind us to add vacation time to our yearly business plans. Thanks to him, the first things I book in my calendar now for next year's business plan are my vacation times. There are two kicks to it, for me.

First, I book it, so I actually have something to look forward to, while working so many hours per day.

Second, I book at least one expensive vacation. That way, I know I REALLY must work seriously, so I can actually afford it. Not bad motivation, right? Be careful, though: If you are not serious about really committing to work, don't do it. You might end up owing more than you can afford.

Find what motivates you. But seriously, you need to have a break from real estate once in a while. If you can't block off a whole week, at least take a few long weekends off! Make sure you block those in the calendar in advance and try to follow through with them.

5. AM I RESPONSIBLE ENOUGH TO KEEP MYSELF ON TRACK?

At one of the training sessions I've attended, at the very beginning in my career here in Canada, I heard that we need to keep ourselves accountable. How do we do that?

They said someone was supposed to check up on us and we were supposed to feel like sh$#, if we didn't accomplish what we said we would.

On my way home from the office, later that day, I was thinking hard. Who can keep me on track? My office? No, I have insubordination issues. If I am "told" to do something I will do quite the opposite. My husband? No, I'll just yell at him.

And then it hit me.

My children are my universe. I would do just about anything and everything for them. As soon as I came home, I called my five-year-old son and my not even three-year-old daughter at that time and sat with them on a couch.

I said: "Mommy is going to work a lot and I will make sure that we still have plenty of fun times together, BUT Mommy needs a favour from you. Every time I come home from work, I need you to ask me, "Mommy, did you make a deal?" And If I did make a deal, we will go to our favourite restaurant at the time, Mandarin. (Don't ask, don't judge!)

That was a great motivation for me, because I would feel so bad to see their disappointed faces if we were not going to Mandarin.

After a few years, we kind of started to go there often, so we needed to change the prize.

Now that I think of it, it was a dumb choice of prize,

but that was the only thing I could think of that would keep their young minds focused and keep "bugging me." I mean keeping me "accountable."

I am not telling you to do the same thing, but you definitely need to find a system to keep you on track. One of the most proven systems is coaching, of course, but if that is not something you are willing to invest in for now, think of who you can buddy with. It can be a new fellow agent too. No need to overthink it. As a matter of fact, maybe it SHOULD be a new agent. That way you both will be helping each other. Even if you don't feel like doing it, you will feel obligated to go to the meeting because the other agent(s) are waiting for you and, best of all, you won't feel "dumb" that you are just a beginner, that your numbers are so low and that you are not as great as someone way more experienced than you.

You can set up a phone call, video, or in-person meeting and review what you have accomplished in the past few weeks. You can do it daily, weekly or every other week, but no less frequently than that.

Here are some "buddy" options:
- A fellow agent. It can be someone who just finished the courses with you.
- Your partner, spouse, children. (Think of a better prize though!)
- Your friend who is in a completely different business but needs some accountability too.

Why is accountability important?

It is simple: If you don't do it, nobody else will do it for you.

If you work in a company and you don't finish your job, they will fire you and have someone else do it. When you are running your own business, if you don't do it, you're in trouble. Do people still lack discipline? Heck yeah. 99.9% of all agents lose focus at some point.

You know that you need to prospect every day, follow up with current clients on a daily basis, follow up with past clients regularly and so much more. If you are not disciplined, you will let leads fall through the cracks and then you will be pissed off and all puzzled. "How come they bought with another agent?" Now you know: Because you didn't follow up with them!

If you don't have anybody to ask you if you did all the daily tasks that you nicely wrote in your calendar (you even colour-coded them) and promised you would do, you will need to be fair to yourself, recognize the signs and ask for help.

If you are absolutely sure there is no way anyone you know will keep you on track, then you should seriously consider investing in coaching. Once you realize that you are paying for that service, it is more likely you will make good use of it too. (I hope!)

6. DO I HAVE MY FAMILY'S SUPPORT?

Starting a new business is not easy and if on top of all the troubles that will come your way you don't have your family support, that journey will likely be short, unsuccessful and painful.

If you are like most people, you've probably researched "how many hours is the average working week for a realtor?" The answers you'll get online are nothing but false!

YOU will determine how many hours you will work. But know one thing for sure, it will NOT be 9-to-5 if you want to succeed. At least it won't be like that until you have a secured and steady business, many years from now.

You will be working more than eight hours a day and you will be working at all hours. Mornings and evenings too.

Many years ago, when we still had those nice "in-person" offer presentations, I was supposed to go and present an offer for my buyers. The property was in Brampton, Ontario, and since the sellers had young children, they requested an offer presentation to start at 9 p.m. I had a good 30-minute drive there, so I had to leave around 8:30 p.m., which was usually bedtime story time for my little girl. As I was all dressed up and about to leave the house, my daughter looked at me from the top of the stairs and asked: "Where are you going, Mommy?" "I am going to work, baby," I answered. She looked at me with those big blue eyes and angel face and sadly asked me back: "Don't they know you have children?"

That was, still to this day, the worst punch in the gut I've ever gotten from this business.

I swallowed my tears, smiled at her and said, "They do know, and they will do their best to let me come home as soon as possible." (Huge lie!) I came home at 1:30 a.m. that night. It was the latest I've stayed for an offer presentation ever.

The sadness was very visible on my face the next morning and I was very close to quitting my job, even though I'd gotten the deal.

My husband tried the best he could to keep it all casual, and act like nothing had happened. He often tried to help, with whatever he could, just to help me with the business.

He would help me drive for showings, to set up the open house signs, sometimes he would even stay with me during open houses (for safety reasons).

He understood the amount of the pressure I was under and, even though the level of his romance was "0" (and that is on the scale 1-10), he has weird ways of showing his love.

He would make sure to ask me if I ate that day, not to forget to get a coat, he would fill out my car with gas if he knew I was fully booked the next day with appointments. And many other things.

He is my best friend, my shoulder when I need it, and a verbal punching bag too! Many times, if I would be stressed out from work, he would be the one I yelled at, over nothing most likely, and he wouldn't say anything. He knew how much pressure I am under, and he also knew that I was not mad at him, but rather just venting out. He would listen patiently until I calmed down. Although, I don't think he actually listened; he probably learned to "tune" me out, until I shut up. Well, after over 33 years together, I know I can still count on him, forever and ever.

If you have a family, try to explain to them what their life will be like for the next few years. And please make sure they fully understand what the sacrifices will be. If they don't know what to expect, it might end up badly.

Unfortunately, I've seen marriages break up over the working hours in real estate. However, I think that was just a last drop in the cup, and not a real reason for a breakup. Still, don't risk it. Be transparent with your significant other and children (if any). Try to involve them in your everyday work too. It helps when they feel included.

When our kids were young, I would have them place stamps on envelopes for mail that I was sending to my database and stick my business cards on the calendars I was sending every Christmas too. I would then "pay" them $5 for their work (for a six- and three-year-old, this was a fortune). They were so happy that they'd "worked" and I'd just saved four to five hours of my time – which I used to prospect more.

If you are on your own, that's OK too. Try to create a system of how to work efficiently. You can ask a colleague, friend, or a family member (sibling, cousin?) to accompany you with open houses and showings, if you are concerned about your safety. You need to know that you are safe at all times. At the appointments and on the road too.

If you are meeting with a person you don't know and you don't have anybody to come with you, have someone you know call you 5 to 10 minutes into your meeting, just to make sure that all is OK. You can have a code word or phrase for "all good" or "trouble."

Now that THEY know and understand your expectations and options and have prepared your family for a "rocky" road, we will need to determine what kind of an agent you will be.

CHAPTER 3

WHAT KIND OF A SALES REPRESENTATIVE ARE YOU?

After you've decided that you really want to proceed with your real estate journey and you (hopefully) have your family's support, you will need to determine what kind of sales representative you want to be.

Regardless of what kind of business you are in, if you are selling something, in my opinion, there are two types of sales representatives. "Transactional" or "Relationship" sales representatives.

TRANSACTIONAL SALES REPRESENTATIVE

Many years back, I was in one of the seminars where I overheard an agent saying: "I wake up every morning as an unemployed person and must work hard to get leads." At first, I wasn't sure what she meant with that statement and then it hit me: She looks like a "Transactional" agent!

The name says it all. Every morning, you wake up and go out prospecting for some leads. Either by doing open houses, cold calls, door knocking, or by placing ads. Whatever.

At one point, you will get a lead. You will happily follow through the transaction process, do a great job (hopefully), and here comes the deal. You meet with them on the closing day with a small closing gift and you move on, searching for another client. Another day of waking up "unemployed," chasing for another lead and another transaction. Does this sound like a hamster on a hamster wheel? This system can work, but, unless you have a "pool" of clients to work with, you will be running like a headless chicken.

WHERE CAN YOU GET THOSE CLIENTS, YOU ASK?

You will need to prospect at the same time as you will be working with buyers and/or sellers. You will need to dedicate time for prospecting every single day. (Actually, you need to prospect every day, regardless of what kind of agent you are. The difference is the time spent and motivation, which I will explain later.) If you do not prospect every day, you will literally be waking up every morning as an unemployed person, chasing the business. That is time-consuming and nerve-racking, if you ask me.

Don't get me wrong, there are some agents who are happy with this system and are perfectly fine with not knowing when they will have their next client and next deal. When the market is good.

The challenge with this system is that even though it might happen that you have many clients to work with at the moment, if the market crashes, your pond filled with leads will dry up. You will wake up one day and that hamster wheel will be staring at you and screaming your name.

Also, prospecting while being busy showing and listing houses is hard. Both – showing homes and preparing properties for sale – literally take many hours. Unfortunately, the day has only 24 of those.

During one of the latest recessions, an experienced agent from asked if I would meet with him. He needed to pick my brain for some marketing ideas. I gladly accepted the invite, hoping there would be some great ideas exchanged. If I have a good marketing idea and that agent has an idea, we will both leave that meeting with two ideas in our books.

When we met, the agent told me his client book was dry and he hadn't had any true leads in a long time. He was trying to do cold calling and open houses, but had no solid leads. Knowing the market conditions, that was exactly what we expected. I suggested that he go back to basics and reach out to his database, to which he replied: "I don't have a database." I was shocked for a second, and when I asked, "how come?" he said he never had anything written in any formal CRM (client retention management, sometimes also called customer relationship management) system. That's another proof of a "transactional" agent. I will repeat again: Nothing is wrong with that system, as long as you are financially ready for the "dry season." Actually, ALL agents must be financially ready for a "dry season" in order to survive market crashes and still be able to provide for their families.

Some realtors will spend thousands of dollars for bus advertising, benches in malls, sports arenas etc. That does often bring them new clients, since the public would have a perception that "this realtor must be very good and rich, if he/she can afford to advertise this much." All of that is fine and dandy, but if the market crashes and you've spent upfront ten of thousands of dollars for those ads and you don't end up making very many deals to cover that cost, you will be in deep doo-doo. Whatever you do, please try to allocate a maximum of up to 30 per cent of your gross income for advertising and marketing. If you spend more than that, you might run into trouble. If you are just starting, then this percentage will be higher for sure, but so will your motivation too, and hopefully you will make enough money to cover that cost.

As a "transactional agent," you will need to be on high alert at all times, always listening to other people's conversations and, what I think is the worst, you will wake up every day as "unemployed," looking for a job.

So, in conclusion, there is nothing wrong with this system, if you have a well-designed and well-executed business plan.

A tip for you, as a transactional agent:
You should have a good financial buffer to keep you afloat for six to nine months, in case you don't have any new deals coming in. Does that sound scary? Well, it is. Dream big, but don't live in the clouds and think you will surely be able to find some business sooner than that. The "dry season" happens to all agents at one point, regardless of the type and experience level.

Now, if this is not your cup of tea, let me see if you would like this cup of coffee called "Relationship agent."

RELATIONSHIP-BASED SALES REPRESENTATIVE

First off, if you thought you would skip prospecting, you are mistaken. You must prospect every day, but not by chasing people you don't know, but rather following up with people you do know (people you have already established a relationship with), which is way easier.

According to the psychology dictionary, a relationship is "a binding, usually continuous association, between individuals wherein one has some influence on feelings or actions of the other."

Our goal is to have some positive influence on the feelings of others, of course. My focus is not on the "feelings," since I hope your clients already feel great about you and the way you handled their home buying/selling transaction.

Rather, I would like to focus on the word "continuous." That is your magic word. This is the water and the sun that the seeds (contacts) you've planted some time ago (in your database) need for them to grow.

Once you establish a positive relationship with a client and/ or lead and you add them to your database, you must **stay in touch continuously**, without having an "end date," to determine when they should buy/sell with you, or send you a lead. You will be providing them with value by sending great information via emails, text messages, phone calls and in-person meetings, without expectation for an instant gratification.

Your goal is that by staying on top of mind with people in your database, you will gently remind them who you are, on a daily basis. That way, THEY will be contacting you when someone needs help with real estate, and not necessarily you having to go and chase them for a referral. It might seem odd, but it is true. You can create scheduled emails, texts and reminders to wish them happy birthday, happy home anniversary and other important occasions. They will be genuinely surprised that you, as a realtor, remember their special days and will gladly talk about you, to their friends and at their parties. How many agents do they know who care THAT much about their clients?

Many years ago, one of my scheduled emails was about the time change, with a reminder to change the batteries in their fire alarms. I usually schedule many auto emails for a whole year in advance, through my CRM software. The "turn back your clocks" email was scheduled in January, to be sent on a Friday before the time change dates in March and in November. When the email was actually sent in November, I received a reply from a client of mine. "Matilda, thank you so much for the reminder! We have completely forgotten about it. BTW, we are thinking that it is time for us to move again. Would you please call me so we can schedule a meeting to discuss our next steps." How cool is that? I didn't ask them if they wanted to buy or sell. I was simply providing them with valuable information. When you establish a relationship with a client and then nurture it like a delicate flower, eventually that flower will bloom – again and again. It will take time for you to establish that relationship, but don't give up. We will be talking about the CRM and life-referring system in the next chapter and hopefully that will help you determine which type of agent you prefer to be.

CHAPTER 4

TYPES OF PROSPECTING

After you decide what kind of real estate agent you want to be, you will need to start working on those leads. Which you don't have. So, let me try and help you with that.

As I mentioned earlier in the book, to prospect with people you know seems much easier than prospecting with people you don't know. But the number of people you know is just a fraction of the number of people you don't know. (Like, the rest of the whole wide world!)

So, since the stats show that people we know will not be too eager to send us leads as soon as we get the licence, we will need to work on those that we don't know.

FYI, people you know will first wait to see if you wash out by the end of the first year. If you are still there next year, they might send you first to someone they know, before they trust you with their own real estate transactions needs. Don't take it personally. You might be nice, intelligent and with all good intentions, but you do not have the experience needed – or at least that is what they are thinking.

They want to see that you gain some experience first, and then, hopefully, they will send you some people. Let me keep repeating the order: Know, like, trust. They do know you, but not professionally, they possibly do like you, but they definitely do not trust you with their real estate needs. At least not yet.

So, instead of repeating my mistake, and being upset that your friends and family are not sending you leads, act as if you know absolutely no one. Clean slate. You've just fallen from Mars and need to introduce yourself to the world. "Hi, I am a Martian and I would like to be your friend – and realtor too."

Based on these groundbreaking rules, you will need to find a way to prospect that will match your personality and preference.

By now, you've heard the types of prospecting a million times, you've probably even been "told" which way to prospect, because "that is the best way." But I am telling you: **Do not listen to that crap!**

YOU need to find a way of prospecting that **YOU** are comfortable doing – as long as you get the results, of course. If you don't like any of the usual ways, then you would either need to invent a new way of prospecting, or to get out of your comfort zone and pick one that scares you the least.

So, listed below is the breakdown of the most common types of prospecting, along with an approximate amount of time and cost you need to spend on them.

Please note that "conversion rate" information is based on an average agent. But I hope you will disregard that portion and that you will be one of the very successful agents in the fields that have a high conversion rate and prove to yourself that you are truly better than the rest of the crowd. YOU are the only one you need to impress, and YOU are the only one you need to prove that you are a great agent. No one else! We've all fallen under that spell that we must prove to others how great we are. But don't. Brush off your ego. The "others" will not be the ones paying your bills and fighting your battles. When you believe in yourself, all is possible.

So, here we go…

TYPES OF PROSPECTING:

LEAST EXPENSIVE
(High Time Demand – Low-To-Medium
  Conversion Rate)
- ☺ Cold Calling
- ☺ Open House
- ☺ Door Knocking
- ☺ Organic Social Media presence

EXPENSIVE
(Low Time Demand – Low-To-Medium
  Conversion Rate)
- ☺ Neighbourhood farming (flyers)
- ☺ Paid Social Media advertising

LOW-TO-MEDIUM EXPENSE
("Pleasant" (For Me And All People-Y Agents)
  – "High-Ish" Time Demand – High Conversion
  Rate)
- ☺ Database
- ☺ Implementation of lifetime referral system

Now, let's dive deeper into these types of prospecting, along with the pros and cons.

COLD CALLING PROSPECTING

This type of prospecting is inexpensive, but will require many hours of you speaking with people you don't know, and the conversion rate will depend on how great you are at the "spiel." I will not be focusing too much on this one in this book, mostly because I am not even sure it is worth doing it anymore, now that most households have cut off the landlines and cellphones have caller ID and "spam" trackers/blockers.

However, if you don't mind calling people and being hung up on, this might be one of the sources of income for you.

You would need a good headset system, access to a phone number list (make sure you are aware of the "do-not-call" list, if it is present in your market area), and off you go.

You would need to know and practise your script and keep dialing. The only thing I would like to add is to maybe do some recon first, before you call.

Just simply calling and asking "are you interested in selling your house this year?" is likely to land you on a loud one "go to hell" before you even use the word "selling."

However, if you select a house that is just listed, or just sold and call the households in that neighbourhood offering some useful information about the listing and market conditions, you might get your foot in the door.

The conversion rate for cold calls is less than two per

cent, but if you create a great followup system, you might stand a chance. However, in my opinion, it's in your best interest that you should not make "cold calling" your only revenue stream.

OPEN HOUSE PROSPECTING

Open houses were, and still are for some agents, one of the best ways to grow a database and to prospect for new leads. It takes time, but at a very low cost.

People who come to visit open houses are already motivated. Well, most of them, at least. Some are just bored people and we call them "tire kickers." They like to kill some time by visiting open houses, eating cookies that agents sometimes provide and taking pens, notepads and other promotional material agents have at their open houses. That's actually not so bad, since your name will be all over town. Free marketing. However, with your expert pre-qualifying 4 W's questions (When, Where, What and Why), I hope you will be able to recognize them from the entrance, give them your goodies and do your best not to waste your time with them.

You must master the 4 W's (don't worry – I'll explain more in Chapter 7), and within a few minutes you should be able to figure out which group they belong to: real clients or the "tire kickers."

TIPS HOW TO HOST A
MEMORABLE OPEN HOUSE:

- Learn everything there is about the house, even if it is not your listing. Speak with the listing agent and get all necessary info about it.
- Learn more about the neighbourhoods, proximity to the parks, public transit, schools and their rankings, etc. (do a drive-by before an open house)
- Research the area and try to figure out the traffic flow. Make sure you strategically post the open house signs (make sure that damn arrow is pointed in the correct direction!).
- Make sure that the home is presentable with all lights on in the house, even though it might be sunny and bright already.
- Houses must have a pleasant room temperature. If it is wintertime, do not keep the house too cold. You want people to have that cozy and warm feeling when they enter the house. In the summer, keep it cool, but not freakishly cold. Some people will just run through the house and leave.
- Avoid any artificial room fresheners. There are many people with sensitivity to smells. Bake, or even just warm some cookies. They work like a charm, unless people are allergic to airborne flour. (heard about that one recently)
- Do NOT play music. You do not know which music your perfect client likes or dislikes. I've seen people rolling their eyes when they enter the house and the music playing is not what they prefer.

Remember, we are trying to appeal to as many buyers as possible.

◎ For the love of God, do NOT watch a sports event on TV, and just tell open house visitors to let you know if they have any questions! I can't even remember how many times I have entered an open house to this scene. This is SO disrespectful toward the visitors. It looks as if you didn't even want to be there!

◎ Point out some features that might not be visible to the naked eye, with a nicely framed poster. i.e. poster with an arrow pointing up to the ceiling, saying "extra insulation done recently," or "potential separate entrance" etc. Please do not use sticky notes. They don't look professional. Remember the saying: "How you do anything is how you do everything." Attention to detail is a must.

◎ Have an easy-to-understand sign-in sheet, with not too many questions. Using an iPad or laptop minimizes the chance of not reading their emails and phone numbers correctly, which is very important for the followup. There are some great apps for open houses too, which go even further, since you will know immediately if they gave you a bogus email. The whole point of hosting an open house is either to sell the property, or to gain a lead. If you can't capture their true information, your time is not well spent.

◎ Have some nut-free, individually wrapped cookies and water bottles available. If you can have them labelled with your information, that's even better.

⊚ You can have a small contest and prizes to be mailed/delivered. For them to qualify, they will need to give you their real names and addresses.

My best friend Deena has a great part of her yearly income based on open house leads. She has gotten buyers, sellers and their families too. All of them. The way she gets them to like her, trust her and do business with her is outstanding. She talks a lot (sorry, Deena, had to say it) but knows how to listen to clients patiently too. She is extremely patient while speaking with people (except when she speaks with me) and they seem to connect with her quickly, so she can sell them on her real estate services. Deena asks all the right open-ended questions, which initiate conversation that will help her to lead them toward the conclusion that they need her to help them, and no one else.

To summarize this part, learn your 4 W's, create a checklist of what you need to have/do for a successful open house, pick up those signs, cookies and water, and off you go this weekend from 2 to 4 p.m.

DOOR KNOCKING PROSPECTING

Door knocking is similar to cold calling: inexpensive but time consuming. If you are targeting the same neighbourhood and doing it repeatedly every few weeks, your face might become familiar to the homeowners and you might even engage in conversation, which hopefully will lead to an appointment. One important thing you should know for door knocking is that you must have some value to provide to homeowners, otherwise it is just a cold call that will end up with the door closing in front of your face. What kind of value to provide? You can combine door knocking with neighbourhood farming and in that case, you would send a flyer with useful information such as market updates for that neighbourhood, most recent sales there and so on, a few days before you actually go door knocking in that area, or you can have those printed out and give them to homeowners when the open the door. We will talk more about this when we dissect the neighbourhood farming portion, but for now let's say you are not farming the neighbourhood.

Your first step would be to select a few streets and neighbourhoods and do some investigation on them. Select a street/neighbourhood and see how many houses are selling there per year. Check the past few years in a row. If there is one, or none, then maybe that will not be a good "prospect" neighbourhood. Some agents might disagree with me, but think of it this way: If there are only one or two sales per year, or even fewer, that means most likely it is a neighbourhood with "forever homes." Those are the houses that people buy to stay for many years and/or even decades. Now, to convince them to sell is definitely not going to be a walk in the park. They love their home, they have been there for so long, have many memories attached to it, and they are comfortable in it. Unless you specialize in the "downsizing" market – in which case I would advise you to check the homes that have had owners for a very long time and focus on those houses only – my advice to you is to skip this neighbourhood.

If you are just starting in the business and trying to grow your database and potential leads, you likely don't have the expertise and experience to convince "forever-home" owners to move, but you could surely ask them for permission to add them to your database and keep in touch with them from time to time. That way, they will get to know you better, and if you provide them with some valuable information at those times, they might even get to trust you a bit. In a long run, that could eventually bring you a few deals. However, if you select a neighbourhood with a higher turnover in sales per year, you have more chance to land a lead.

Neighbourhoods with smaller properties such as townhouses, semi-detached and smaller detached homes with a one-car garage are more likely to move sooner than owners of large homes. Their families have grown and they need that extra bedroom or parking space. Their jobs have changed, they need a better school district or whatever. Learn your script, practise objection handling, and off you go.

TIP 1:

Select neighbourhoods with high sales turnover and learn pros and cons about the neighbourhood. It might give you an idea what the homeowners would like to have and what is missing in that neighbourhood. Find a neighbourhood that has those missing puzzle pieces, so when you door knock, recommend those neighbourhoods instead. Oh, and make sure you have some listings to show them, or most recent sales there, so they can see how moving is not such a bad and expensive idea (hopefully).

TIP 2:

> Always have some "goodie bags" to give away that are NOT just your pens and calendars. Those will likely go straight to the garbage bin. However, if you have a fridge magnet with cooking measurement conversions (with your info on it, of course), it is more likely to be kept. In our multicultural country, that is absolutely one thing that is very likely to stay on the fridge door, or handy in a drawer, for a long time.

TIP 3:

> Don't target too many houses per day. It can get exhausting, your energy will change and, believe me, the homeowners can sense when your energy is low. Instead, make a goal to door knock on only 10 doors per day, or until you get one client's permission to add them to your database. Designate only an hour per day for this kind of prospecting and implement some other type of prospecting for another hour.

ORGANIC SOCIAL MEDIA PROSPECTING

Organic social media prospecting is free and can be a lot of fun. Maybe too much fun. Actually, it can be so much fun that you could lose focus easily as to why you were there in the first place. Forget looking at cute pets chasing their tails, adorable babies sneezing at their parents' faces etc. You are there to post valuable information, like your friends/clients posts and to comment on them too. You must be genuinely engaged in online conversation, so people can notice you. Feel free to give real estate advice, WITHOUT pointing out that you are a realtor. Someone once asked about the best place to buy moving boxes and I just told them where I got mine. Nothing more, nothing less. Just be present.

Join different groups and, let me repeat again, do NOT toot your own horn. What do I mean by that? If someone online is asking for a great realtor in your marketplace, the worst thing you can do is to say: "pick me!" Instead, make sure you team up with family, friends, clients and colleagues and as soon as that kind of post shows up, you have THEM mention your name as a great and trustworthy agent (assuming you are actually one of those, of course).

Speak with them in advance and tell them that you might need a favour from them in the future, and make sure they are available and willing to do so. If there is more than one person recommending you, you will have an even bigger chance of landing that client.

A few years back, someone asked about a realtor in my area and a few friends recommended me. I thanked them in a comment and then privately messaged the client offering my help, along with a Google review page and my website links. That person only needed help with a rental, having just arrived in the country. Even though I do not deal with tenants much, I helped them. Less than two years later, they bought a nice home that landed me almost $27,000 in commission. Pretty cool, right? The key principle here is that I stayed in touch with them all that time. I will explain how further down in the book, when we talk about nurturing your database.

For someone who has been using computers since 1993, it was not too hard for me to learn how to create posts on different social media platforms, but knowing what is trending, which keywords to use and at what time of the day to do those posts was no easy task. It still isn't. Thankfully, everything is now explained on YouTube, so feel free to browse and explore what a good post consists of, how to gain followers and more.

For me, social media is my online business card. We know that whenever someone recommends a business, the first thing we do is we Google them. If they are not present online, to us they are likely "not good." It is a very wrong assumption, since I know some great agents who do not have a heavy presence online. But they will soon become obsolete unless they pick up their game. If they are not capable, or willing to study and do the legwork on social media, they could hire an assistant for it. There are so many kids out there who can do it for a fraction of the time it would take us to do, and it won't break the bank.

If you prefer to do it yourself, to be money conscious, work backwards. Make sure you know your audience first. Know who you are targeting to be your clients and then focus on those platforms only.

Follow successful agents on different platforms and see what they are doing. It might give you some ideas on topics and ways to organize your social media presence. But never copy their posts. Customize them to reflect your own professional standards, ideology and theme.

A few years ago, I was in one of the great seminars about social media and I got too excited. I had a profile on

Facebook, including a fan page, LinkedIn and Instagram, but I wasn't on Tik Tok. That one became a hit of the year. Wanting to be up to date with social media trends, I asked my assistant to create me an account. I started creating short videos, which she then edited. They looked cute, but they were taking plenty of my time and energy in creating them. A few months later, I started receiving inquiries, which mostly sounded like this: "Hey, I am a student and I'm looking to rent a room." After receiving quite a few of those, I realized I was on the wrong social media platform. I was screaming to the phone, "Your parents should be my clients for buying and selling, and not you for a room renting!" Once I said that out loud, the lightbulb went on! "I am on the wrong platform!" Who do I want to be my clients? What age distribution are they? Which social media do they use (if any)?

After triple checking my database and my past deals, I realized that Facebook and LinkedIn are where my clients hang out, and their millennial children are likely on Instagram, so I must be there too. Why, you ask? Well, when the kids say they are thinking of buying/selling real estate, their parents, who are on my platform, of course, will say: There is a great real estate agent we know. What will be the first thing those kids do? Yup, they will check my online presence. Since I'm on Instagram too, they might see me as a "relevant" agent to help them.

FYI, I am NOT good with Instagram. I just have a great social media assistant. However, this doesn't mean that you have to be on these platforms. You must review your clientele and who is your target market, and then focus on those.

TIPS FOR A SOLID FREE
ONLINE PRESENCE:

- ⊚ Take some online free educational sessions on social media
- ⊚ Decide which age group you would like to target
- ⊚ Focus on those social media platforms only

This will save you some time and energy to focus on tasks that are productive and that matter.

NEIGHBOURHOOD FARMING

This is very similar to door knocking, but you would be focusing all your energy and marketing toward one neighbourhood only. You would do door knocking, cold calling, open houses and neighbourhood events only in this area. Your taglines would include wordings such as "your neighbourhood realtor" or "your neighbourhood specialist" (if allowed to use word specialist by the boards), or something similar.

Usually, neighbourhood farming includes sending flyers regularly, every two to three weeks. Then you should call the homeowners as a followup on those flyers, or you can do door knocking too.

You can offer to sponsor street parties, local kids' sport/ dance clubs. You can deliver some goodies each season, such as pumpkins in the fall, honey and teabags in the winter, plant seeds in the spring and more. It is always to the same neighbourhood, preferably on the same days of the week, and people should start to notice you. This is a very lengthy prospecting process, and it is not likely it will result in sales quickly. Sometimes it takes over a year to generate a solid lead. Again, they will need to get to KNOW you, then LIKE you. And once you gain their TRUST, you should start seeing the results. Being a "neighbourhood agent" doesn't mean you will reject other areas' buyers and sellers, but this might be a sword with two very sharp edges. If you get well known as an agent from one neighbourhood, it will be harder for people to refer you out of the area, since those referees might not see you as an expert in their areas and property types. So, unless the area you select has a very high density of units, carefully evaluate the area and see if it will be a good source of income for you.

TIP:

> You can do neighbourhood farming with all those ideas I gave you earlier as one of your sources of income. However, think twice whether you should use taglines such as "neighbourhood agent" in your marketing material.

Important: This prospecting, if done properly, can be very costly and not many startup businesses can afford that. Please make sure you review all costs tied to this type of prospecting to see if you are better focusing on some other prospecting option.

PAID SOCIAL MEDIA ADS

I remember the "old days" (which weren't that long ago) when we printed our real estate ads in local newspapers and specialized real estate magazines. That was a really expensive type of prospecting. But if you knew how to properly structure the ads and how to convert the phone call to a lead by using your strong skills in probing those 4W questions, which would convert to a client, you could make a really good income from it.

I know I sure did. Then social media became popular, many people stopped buying hardcopy newspapers and turned over to online options. Google, Facebook and Twitter started running ads, followed by Snapchat and Tik Tok. Most of us stopped paying big bucks to local newspaper providers and focused on some free and paid ads through major social network platforms.

But who do you target with your ads? You will need to know before you spend your money on paid ads online. They are not inexpensive, either. If you are targeting ages 40 to 65ish, you should probably be on Facebook. I don't think those ads would have a great result on Tik Tok or Snapchat, since that age group is not likely to be very active on those platforms. I am not sure that even Instagram would work well for this age group.

But if you are targeting 25 to 40ish, Instagram might be a better option. Another thing you need to know is which type of properties you are trying to advertise and who would be a buyer for those homes.

For example, if you are selling a $2-million house, placing ads on Tik Tok and Instagram is probably not a good investment of your time and money. Why? Well, to go back to the age group, how many 25-year-olds can actually afford a $2-million house?

Many agents pay social media companies to maintain their social media presence, but please make sure you are tightly following up with them if you do, to make sure they are properly promoting you and your business to the appropriate target market by using the right social media platforms and keywords. Those ads must reflect you, your personality and your way of doing business.

When I first hired a social media assistant, she was doing a great job, until one day my best friend texted me saying: "yo, since when are you a yoga fan?" I love martial arts; I am loud and never sit still, and all my clients and friends know that. Yoga is absolutely not something that I would do and create posts with it. I instantly called my assistant, told her to take the post down from the social media platforms, and then we had a lengthy meeting where I got her to know me, the way I do business and my lifestyle better, for the future reference.

This type of prospecting can be a bit less expensive than neighbourhood farming, but it can still cost a good chunk of money. The biggest problem I see with both neighbourhood farming and social media is that the conversion rate is usually low and instant results are rare too.

TIP 1:

> When running an ad, make sure you check the ad analytics regularly and follow the trend of visits, likes and plays (if video). Those will show you when your audience is most active online and then always schedule those ads, and regular posts too, at those specific times.

TIP 2:

> If you don't have listings, as mentioned earlier in the book, you can always ask your colleagues to advertise their listings. But you don't need to be limited to your colleagues only. Some real estate boards have a field in their systems if the listing agent is open to allowing others to advertise their listings. That can be a great pool of listings for you to advertise, with listing agents' permission, of course.

DATABASE – CRM

What is a database/CRM? If you google the definition, you will get the same answer, with many different fancy and some not-so-fancy descriptions. A database is an organized collection of data, set up for easy access, management and updating.

My plain English version of it: A database is a client care system, with all information you can get on your clients, friends, family, leads, colleagues, lawyers, inspectors, plumbers and everyone else who knows you by your first name. Beside the usual – names, phone numbers and emails – you should definitely have their family members' information too, including children and pets. What are their likes, dislikes, favourite foods, places? Any personal information you can get. I know it seems a lot like stalking, but it is not. (It will get clearer, just keep reading). That information will help you establish rapport and show them that you care about them. Remember, you are here to help people and not just to sell real estate.

You should buy a CRM specifically designed for realtors, and that is one of the expenses I strongly advise you not to skip.

If you use your database followup system to the best of your capabilities, the return on it could range from 10 percent to 25 percent – and if you master it, even more than that. For starters let's say you get a 10 percent return. If you have 100 people in your database, you should get 10 deals per year. That doesn't mean 10 of the people in your database will buy or sell with you, but it surely means some of them might deal with you and some others might refer you some business, and that should total 10 deals.

HOW DO YOU GET THOSE DEALS?

As I mentioned earlier, for people to trust you, they will need to get to know you first, and like you too.

By providing them with useful information throughout the year and staying at the top of their minds throughout the year, via emails, snail mails, personal calls and face-to-face meetings, you should achieve that. You should treat your database as your gold mine. Make sure you follow up with people regularly, and not necessarily offer them your real estate services only. Of course you can share your newest listings, providing them with market updates, but you should also offer them valuable information in regard to improving their homes, regular maintenance, recommending them great services and contractors, and even more importantly, show that you care. Call them on their birthdays, send them an email, or drop by with a gift for their special home anniversary, etc. People like to see that you are there for them not just when you need them to buy and sell real estate. All these touches will lead your database members to like you and trust you and when next time someone asks about a good realtor, your name will easily come to their minds.

HERE IS THE LIST OF PEOPLE WHO SHOULD BE IN YOUR DATABASE:

- ☺ Your family members
- ☺ Your friends
- ☺ People who know you by your first name
- ☺ Services/businesses you cross paths with or refer to
- ☺ Fellow agents from different trading areas
- ☺ Networking and social groups

Keep checking and updating your database regularly. Create different groups in it for your "A" clients, "B" clients, "strategic alliance" and so on. Create it in a way that you will easily understand and use it and don't worry if it doesn't match what other people do.

CHAPTER 5

HOW TO CONNECT AND BUILD RAPPORT WITH A CLIENT

Now, let's see how you can gain that trust, by not just doing your job professionally – that is what is expected anyway – but also by going above and beyond in being interested in them and remembering them.

When you meet with a lead/client, for the first time, try to establish rapport, some common ground. Find something in common and build on it. You will need to try to mimic their behaviour, the way they talk, their preferences etc. You should get familiar with personality types, such as Color Personality Assessment or DISC. (It's Googling time. Find those tests and run a personality assessment on yourself first. You will learn a lot about yourself.) I am sure there are a few more out there, but these two are easy to understand and implement in your everyday business.

In plain English, there are four main personality types and we have parts of them all, but one or two of those types are more dominant then the others. The sooner you determine what kind of personality a person you speak with is, the sooner you can start mimicking their behaviour, which should lead to building that rapport faster. If someone just entered your open house and started asking questions about the roof, furnace, windows, you should answer those questions ASAP, and add a few more facts to it too that they didn't even think of asking: Roof done 2021 and had new insulation added at the same time; furnace and air conditioning in 2018, but they have a plan that provides maintenance four times a year. You should definitely not tell them: "I don't know that, but isn't the sunset we have from the living room simply breathtaking?" This comment just cost you a potential deal and/or a new client.

For people who are very compassionate and imaginative, make sure you DO mention that sunset, the great schools and friendly neighbours. You've probably heard the statement "it takes seven seconds for a buyer to either love or hate the house." Well, you will have exactly seven seconds, or less, to recognize the personality of a visitor and to try to win them over in the next few minutes they will spend at the open house, or that buyer you just met, or that seller that you just had a listing presentation for. The sooner you recognize that clients' personality, the sooner you will be able establish rapport, and the bigger chance for you to land that deal, buyer and/or seller.

Many years ago, I hosted an open house on one of my listings. It was a slow day and I decided to chat with people more than usual. I was about to finish the open house when a young lady entered the home. After the usual prequalifying questions, we'd determined that this home was not suitable for her sister, who was coming back home from Italy, and that she should look to rent instead of buying for some time, before she becomes eligible for financing. I also noticed that she has a dominant "blue" personality. (People with dominant "blue" personality care a lot about others and want to contribute to everything they are a part of. Relationships are important to them. They are compassionate and sincere) I thanked her for her time and as I was escorting her to the door, I noticed her purse, which she had left next to the entrance. I really liked it and we engaged in conversation about purses, for the next 20 minutes or so. I learned that we had so much in common, including purses and shoes, but I'd also learned that she lived close by in a condo she owned. I didn't ask anything about the condo, just threw out a few lines about the complex and what I know and like about it, and some not-positive feedback I get from buyers when we look there. I also gave her some tips about renting in the area, and she asked me if I could help her sister. Me being me, and not being able to say no to a person with great purse taste, I promised to help.

Soon enough, we did find her sister a great home, and during that process of looking for a rental, I got to meet most of her family too. After the closing, I did what I always do. Add the new names to my database, along with their birthdays, daughter's name, daughter's birthday, hobbies and so on. I made sure they got my Christmas card, my newsletter, calendar AND invitations to my bowling and movie morning events, and just "checked in" with the sister a few times a year, to see if they need any help settling in their new home. After some time, this woman called me out of the blue and said she was thinking of selling her condo and buying a house and would like to see how I could help her.

To wrap up my "purse story," and how being able to recognize people's personalities and implement that knowledge into conversation, here is the result: I sold her condo, she bought a large house with me, we sold it a few years after that, and bought another condo for her. End result: one purse "like" conversation, around $50K in commissions. Not bad, isn't it? Be interested in people and their lives, try to find common ground by implementing personality test questions, and relate to them. Ask questions, pay attention, and I am sure you will find something in common with them sooner or later.

CHAPTER 6

WHO IS YOUR CLIENT?

When you start in business, we all know that you won't be too "picky" about who your clients will be. But you should still start thinking about it and make sure you have at least some clarification on who you would prefer to work with, and advantages and disadvantages of both. We will deep dive into those very soon.

First off, will you be dealing with one type of real estate, as in residential, or commercial?

A lot of people say they will do both. To which, if you could see my face right now, it would read "what BS!" You might know the basics of both, but you will never be a true specialist in both fields, and you may hurt your clients in ways you can't even imagine.

In plain English, it's like an obstetrician saying: "I can do a double bypass heart surgery, no worries." I am sure that an obstetrician had some classes about the double bypass during their medical school, but it is not what they should be doing, and are specialized to do, on a daily basis. Would you let an obstetrician operate on your heart, or maybe do a root canal?

You can't be a "Jack of all trades" regardless of what someone might say. Actually, yes, you can be a "Jack of all trades," but I doubt you will be a "specialist" in it. As the old saying goes: "Jack of all trades, master of none."

So, for the purposes of this book, we will assume you will be specializing in residential real estate.

WHO WILL BE YOUR CLIENT?

Here are some of your options:

- First-time homebuyers
- Mover-uppers
- Downsizers
- Investors

Since you are just starting, you will likely say, "my client will be – whoever comes to me" (I know that's exactly what I said when I first started). And that is perfectly fine. However, that doesn't mean you shouldn't start thinking which group you would like to work with the most.

Even though I have been in the business for a long time, I still love working with buyers. Seven out of 10 senior agents will tell you that they prefer sellers. They will likely tell you that by working with sellers, they have more time to work with several clients at the same time. But still, my two cents on that are that those agents are either too lazy to drive around showing houses, or really don't like seeing people on a daily basis. But hey, if it works for them, who am I to say differently?

Working with buyers is much more work, for sure, compared to working with sellers, but the bond you gain while working with buyers gives you more chances for them to get to know you well. While working with buyers, you will likely get to meet their family and friends too, who will show up to give them their "expert "advice on the homes we are seeing. If you play your cards right, you might have just picked up a few more future clients too.

Remember, any and every client will need to get to know you first, then like you and only then will they trust you, which hopefully will result in doing business with you. (Unless you screw up somewhere along this process). Don't worry, I have absolutely no doubt you will screw up at least a few times in your career. It has happened to all of us. And if someone says differently, they are not just lazy, but they are liars too!

FIRST-TIME HOMEBUYERS

My biggest passion are first-time homebuyers. If you ask 99% of all real estate agents in the world, they will start screaming, kicking and vomiting at this statement. Well, again, I am speaking about myself and you should definitely choose for yourself who you would most like to work with. And don't let anyone tell you that you are wrong. Screw them! Remember, if you do what you love, your work will not feel like work, but rather a joyful life ride that will secure you a great wealthy life and a nice retirement nest.

Why do I like working with first-time homebuyers? I think my maternal instincts kick in. After hearing so many horror stories of buyers getting screwed over big time, I feel a need to protect them from getting taken advantage of. I know it seems selfish, but when I see how happy they are when they get the keys, and how much they appreciate me and my help, my heart jumps for joy and it makes me feel like a superhero.

In early 2011, I had first-time homebuyers I will remember forever, and I am sure they will remember me too – for good reason, of course. The husband had just arrived from Europe and they had been living with two very young children at his wife's parent's house. We'd looked for a suitable house for them and lost quite a few homes in multiple-offer situations. One evening, a new listing showed up and we went immediately to see it. I had an offer typed and printed, just in case we liked it, so we could act fast.

Sure enough, they loved it. I told my clients we should not wait. At that time, it took longer for houses to be uploaded on a public realtor's site, and the biggest advantage was that the agent didn't yet have it listed at the local real estate board. We had literally stayed there waiting for the sellers to return home, and the listing agent to come too, so I could present the offer. After some negotiation, I managed to secure the deal and when I walked to the car and delivered the happy news to them, he hugged his wife and started crying. Seeing them hugging and crying together is by far the biggest reward I've had in my real estate career. I had many great deals done, negotiated huge discounts for buyers, got ridiculously high prices for the sellers, but this is the one I will always remember. It will always be my most memorable and dearest deal ever.

Now, do you want to deal with this much drama on a daily basis? It's your call.

Believe me, working with first-time homebuyers is like taking a child for its first day to school. You need to hold their hand the whole time, watch for them not to wander too far from the road, wipe their tears when they fall and make sure you bring them home safely. My clients often recognize me as a realtor and a shrink too. As I said before, this doesn't mean that you have to work with first-time homebuyers. This is merely a road map for you what to expect when working with them. Not all of them will be too demanding, but a good number of them will. The better you understand them, the better you will be able to navigate this "walk to school."

MOVER-UPPERS

Do you love challenges?

Working with mover-uppers is like juggling five pins in the air, while riding a unicycle – on barbed wire!

So, what should you expect when working with mover-uppers? You absolutely must understand their needs and wants, not a hundred per cent, but a million per cent!

(Yeah, I know that doesn't exist in math, but it does exist in real estate, so bear with me.) You have to create a plan that will match their criteria to the letter. Do not try to take shortcuts. Do not believe that "maybe" they will not be so upset if they don't get what they want. Make sure you explain to them all the risks, present them with all possible scenarios and results and let them choose the level of risk they are willing to take. And make sure you have that in writing. The beauty about working this way is, once they choose the scenario, and you, of course, repeat all pros and cons for it, they will have no reason to doubt you or blame you if the end result is not to their expectation.

For example, if they tell you they will move to another house only if they find that specific one that they love, in the neighbourhood they love, then you shouldn't push them to sell their current house first. If you get greedy and hope they will settle for something else when you get them a ridiculously high price on their home, even though you get them an amazing price they will have that bitter taste in their mouths for not finding their dream home. Believe me, they will not be your "advocates" and they will not be sending you new business. Remember what we mentioned earlier in the book: You are here for the long haul. Be patient and the rewards will come.

Mover-upper clients are more common once you are in the business for a few years and your past clients are ready to move to a larger home. However, someone could call you from an ad, or a referral, to sell and buy, and if you never worked with them before that might be even harder, so please make sure they understand the process well.

One of the pitfalls is to think it will be easier if they already know, like and trust you. Explaining the process to them might be easier, but it is riskier too. They might just go with the flow and do whatever you say without actually thinking if that is truly the scenario they want. If the end result doesn't pan out, guess who's fault it will be? Yours! Please make sure you explain the process and all risks to them, as if you were seeing them for the first time in their lives.

Many years ago, friends of mine decided to use my services as their realtor. Since I have known them for many years, I skipped all the formalities. We were going to the same parties, dancing, laughing, and joking around all the time, and it wasn't until I was negotiating a deal for them that I got that slap in the face. In the middle of negotiation, I stopped my friends from making a mistake and after I explained to them why that would be a crucial mistake, my friend looked at me and said: "Wow, never in a million years would I have thought that you knew that much." I know that she meant it as a compliment, but to me that was a real hard punch in the face. Since then, each and every time I do a listing or buyers' presentation to someone I know personally or professionally, regardless of how many times we have done a deal together, I will go through the whole presentation as if I was seeing them for the very first time.

If you are meeting with someone who doesn't know you, and you explain thoroughly the process, pros and cons of each scenarios in buying and selling at the same time, you should gain an instant respect from them, since you will show them that you care for them and their success, and are not just showing them the red carpet and rose petals. Those thorns that you pointed out gave you an outstanding advantage, since you have a 70 percent chance that other agents they interviewed before you didn't mention any of those negative impacts. My advice to you is don't be afraid to say potential problems to a client. A problem is not a problem if there is a solution. So, point out any potential hiccup and then show them how you will help them deal with it.

DOWNSIZERS

Our dear downsizers are special too. If you thought there is a type of a client who will not be demanding, who will not need you to be a shrink too, you are gravely mistaken. Downsizers are people who likely have been living in the same home for a few decades or more and they need or want to move to something smaller that doesn't need so much maintenance and work. All that is good. We know for sure they will like some specific area, closer to their children maybe, or the water or something else. We know they will either want a bungalow, a smaller townhouse, or even a condo. All nice and dandy. You know their budget is awesome, likely having very little or no mortgage at all, so no need to worry if the closing on the sale of their house is not matching.

But here comes the hammer in the head: "I can't fit my custom-made dining table in this condo." "Where will my piano go?" and to wrap it up: "I can't fit my king-size bed in this bedroom." It is hard for them to part with the three reclining chairs they have in their family room now and all the other unnecessary furniture they gathered over the time. How do you solve this problem? Yeah, drinking won't help. We need to kind of "play" with their brains. Here are some useful tips:

TIP 1:
Make sure the pre-listing process starts a minimum six months in advance.

TIP 2:
Try to find a "comrade" in someone they trust and will listen to.

TIP 3:
Ask them to slowly sell/give away all that bulky furniture you know it will be impossible to place in a new, much smaller place. Use staging as an excuse: "We need to stage it to appeal to more buyers and bring you top dollar."

This way, you will avoid all those questions that have given me, and so many other realtors, nightmares. Planning ahead and working with downsizers can be really nice and entertaining. I usually love listening to their stories (as long as they speak fast). I've learned so much city history while showing them properties.

INVESTORS

Simply explained, a real estate investor is a person or corporation that invests money in purchasing and selling properties, counting on property value appreciation, and/or renting the same for cashflow. Usually, it all looks great on paper. However, what people forget to do is to calculate the usual expenses and losses that will come their way. This is where you, as an expert realtor, have to point those out and to advise them about all the good and bad that is involved in investing. Believe me, if you do that, they will appreciate you way more than if you only do a sugar-coating speech.

My definition of an investor is: M-M-S, short for Math-Money-Stomach

The way I see it, the investor must have these three major strengths:

Firstly, they must be **great at math**. And I don't mean "I'll use the computer and calculator" good. I mean extremely good with math, so they can properly calculate all initial and ongoing costs and prepare for an exit plan too. I am sure you are thinking now, why them, if they can get an accountant for that? The reasoning behind this madness is to make their lives and yours easier.

Let's say they call you all excited, saying they have found a property on the market for a long time that has already lowered its price three times and they hope they can lower it even more. "What a great deal we can make" they say, and you are then trying to explain to them that it is not a good investment, due to a bad ROI (return on investment). You start throwing numbers at them and they look at you as if you are speaking a long-dead foreign language. What a waste of time and energy. They will be upset with you because you don't want to show it to them, and you will be angry that they do not understand that you are saying it for their own good.

Secondly, they must have **available funds**. Not just for the down payment, but also a buffer to sustain a minimum of six months without any rent. This is where most rookie investors fail. People look at the equity in their home and decide they have enough to put as a downpayment on an investment property. They get all excited and go out and purchase one, without doing the proper math. All goes well on closing, they take over the property and expenses.

The market slows down and the first month goes by with no tenants. They have to pay for all expenses for carrying that property, along with all expenses for their own home. They pull out money from their savings, if they are lucky to have any, or borrow against their credit card, which is very bad. The second month comes along, the property is still not rented and the vicious cycle continues. Do you see where I am going with this?

Therefore, the next time you hear someone say they can buy an investment property because they have some savings and/or equity in their home, please make sure you educate them about the "buffer" part. They will appreciate you for that.

Lastly, an investor must have a **great stomach**. And I don't mean six-pack abs, I mean a great stomach to deal with the stress and calculated risks (and some not calculated risk too). Many investors lose a lot of money if they pull the plug too early, or don't calculate well their expenses before getting into it, and know how to deal with the problems of tenants that are likely to happen at some point.

Your job will be to deliver them the harsh truth, that if they are not good with numbers, and/or they don't have someone to run the numbers for them, they will be at great risk to lose some money. The same rule applies to you as well, as a realtor who is helping the investors. If you are not great with numbers, if you don't know how to calculate appreciation (believe me, I've seen and tried to help some agents with that task), working with investors might not be the best choice for you.

If you really want to dip into that market, simply make sure you have a great accountant on your "speed dial" (yes, I'm that old, and for you "youngsters" - have their number saved in your favourites), who is willing to help you with clients. Maybe you can work on a referral system and they can become a crucial part of your Strategic Alliance. You bring investors to them as clients, and they help you assure that the whole process is done well for the investors.

What do investors want? Positive cashflow and great appreciation. That will be possible only if you know how to select properties that have that potential. You will need to explain to your clients about initial costs, ongoing expenses and making sure that the property has a "fast flip" potential. I will not go into explaining these to you, since that could be a book on its own, but if you decide that investors are the clients you want to work with, make sure you get very well educated about these items. Get connected with accountants. Learn the rules of trading with investment properties and government responsibilities. Learn as much as you can.

Make sure you advise your clients to select the accountants who deal a lot with investment properties, and not to go for the cheapest one! That can bite them in the rear, and they can end up losing money, or not gaining as much as they thought, on their investment properties. Investors have to have a mindset that they need to give in order to gain. If they have the mentality of just getting money, without any expense, please tell them not to proceed with investing in real estate, before they get hurt. Again, we all know who will be blamed for a failure.

CHAPTER 7

CLIENT PREQUALIFICATION

THE 4 W'S

Finally, we are at my favourite, and I would say one of the most important backbones in real estate business. Regardless of whether you are working with a buyer or a seller, investors or downsizers, you will need to do some pre-qualifications before you even consider them to be your clients. Remember, you should choose your clients and not the other way around.

The first step for all your clients is a bulletproof formula of **4 W's**.

What is that, you ask?

When I joined a brokerage in Mississauga, I loved attending meetings and seminars. I was eager to learn as much as I could about real estate trading in Canada.

On one of the great seminars the office provided, I heard one of the presenters saying the following sentence, which became my favourite mantra:

"If there is no **WHEN, WHERE, WHAT** or **WHY**, it's time to say goodbye!" ☺

- ☺ "**WHEN** do you need to move/sell?"
- ☺ "**WHERE** do you need to go?"
- ☺ "**WHAT** kind of property are you looking for?"
- ☺ "**WHY** are you selling/buying?"

As soon as I went back to my office that day, I created small note-size forms with six rows and two columns. And every time someone would call me for a property inquiry, I would take that piece of paper and start by asking following questions:

Name	
Phone number	
WHEN (do they need to move/sell)	
WHERE (do they need to go)	
WHAT (kind of property are they looking for/selling)	
WHY (are they selling/buying)	

I had those small forms on my desk in the office, on my home office desk, in my car, in my husband's car, I even had them in every purse I had too. The "4 W's" system has become a pillar of my daily business. The phone rings, I take a pen and the form and off I go with asking those questions.

You need to pre-qualify the leads so you know how serious they are about buying or selling, and/or what is their urgency to do it. They should have an answer to at least one of those questions. Based on their answers, you will know how "hot" the lead is and whether you should work with them or simply say "bye-bye" to them.

You can divide leads in A/B/C or 1/2/3 based on the urgency. Or use whichever method you like, as long as you can distinguish the urgency of the lead. Call them rabbit, horse and snail, if you like. It is not important, as long as you can recognize which type the prospect is.

Here is what I use (and probably a majority of agents out there too):

> "**A**" lead for someone who will buy /sell within one to three months,
> "**B**" lead for someone who will buy/sell within six to nine months and
> "**C**" or "cold" lead for someone who is planning to act in a year or later.

Lately, I've added another group. It is something between "now and never" and I call it group "**S**" – surprise. I have at least a few of those deals each year.

Based on the answers you get from the prospect, you should be able to place them in appropriate categories, and make sure you follow a contact system that you will design for each group (how often will you follow up with them so they don't slip through the cracks and go with someone else).

If they say they need to move by the end of the next month, that should be a solid "A" lead and you will need to act fast.

If they didn't have a solid answer on at least one of those four questions, they were not serious. (They probably just liked your picture and were bored.)

Here are some examples of the answers to "4 W's" questions:

"A" LEAD

Qualifying:
Someone approaches you by saying they have just changed jobs and must relocate to the city you work in, within the next 45 days. They have a great "Why" (relocation), a "When" (45 days) and a "Where" (your city). Three out of four "W's." It is very likely that if they have these three "W's," they will likely know "What" they need too. That is a great "A" lead.

Action for Buyer Clients:
Urgency is there and therefore you will need to act fast. You'd better have a few mortgage providers, inspectors and lawyers available to recommend to your client. If not, it is not the end of the world. Make sure you ask your trusted network – your broker of record/manager, colleague you know who will steer you in the right direction or, a last resort, post on real estate forums groups on social media you are part of. I personally would ask all of them, and then

compare the notes. You should give a few names to your clients anyway. They should be able to choose someone they feel more connected to.

Actions for Seller Clients:
If they are Sellers, moving out urgency remains.

> **Step 1:** You should have contractors, stagers and photographers ready to act fast. If you have a system in place for all scenarios, it will be much easier and the chance for an error is minimized. When I say systems, I mean a checklist of all procedures and steps for the homebuying and homeselling process, along with the names, phone numbers and in which order they need to be addressed. Another beauty is that, even if you are not there, whoever is helping you with the transaction can follow the steps and your clients will likely have a smooth and nice home buying/selling experience.

> **Step 2:** Check if they will be renting or buying in the new location. If it is out of your working area, connect them with a realtor you trust, or ask your office colleagues and friends for a trustworthy one. Make sure you speak with the agent first, to ensure they will treat your clients with the respect and professionalism they deserve, and ask if they will co-operate. You can still earn a referral fee from that transaction.

"B" LEAD

Qualifying:

A young couple contacted you saying they've just found out they will have a baby next spring. They are too excited now and, since they are renting a place, they would like to welcome their new addition to the family in a new home. They have a "Why" (growing family) and a "When" (next spring), which is great. You can work together to finalize the other W's and create a safe plan for them, if possible.

Action: You must stay in touch with them at least once a month (or more often, by providing some valuable information, which I explained before) and slowly get them ready for the purchase. If they want to move in before the baby is born, then you would start looking to purchase a few months before the baby's due date, with the closing to be closer to the time they are expecting the baby, or whichever is their preference.

If that happy couple are sellers, and live in a small condo, you will pull out that awesome "homeselling checklist" we've just explained earlier, and start the process of creating a safe sell/buy plan for them, according to their lifestyle and needs. Let me repeat one thing over and over again, you MUST follow up with them regularly, or otherwise, they might go out on a limb and visit an open house. If you are not on top of their mind, they might completely forget that you exist and purchase on the spot with another agent.

"C" LEAD

Buyers example: A young professional recently immigrated to Canada. He has just started a new full-time job and is working on establishing his credit history and saving for a down payment. He would like to buy something in a year or so.

Actions for Buyer Clients:

> **Step 1:** Explain in detail the buying process, rules and regulations in your province, along with how you are different from other agents, and why they need you.

> **Step 2:** Connect them with a mortgage provider you trust, so they can create a fast-track plan on how to establish the credit report.

> **Step 3:** Follow up with the buyers at least once a month, by providing value to them. Make sure you speak with them and meet in person at least once every few months. They must get to know you and like you, in order to trust you and do business with you.

Sellers example: A family contacted you saying they are waiting for their youngest child to finish high school and to go to university. Just after that happens, they will be ready to sell their current home and downsize to a smaller unit. That will be in a year or so.

Action for Seller Clients:

Step 1: You should meet with them and create a long-term plan. Evaluate their home, see if anything should be improved in it and give them a "to-do" list. I usually suggest meeting with a seller six to nine months before listing the house for sale. This way, they can do it slowly, without rushing and putting much pressure on them, financially and mentally too.

Step 2: If there is some work to be done, that will be a great excuse for you to follow up with them regularly, maybe once a month. Connect them with contractors you trust and make sure they do deliver what is promised.

Step 3: If there is no need to improve anything, you still must maintain the connection, on a monthly basis, by providing value to them. Do regular "market health checkups." Call them and meet with them every few months with some "goodie bags" for the upcoming holidays etc. Otherwise, someone else might come in and take them away from you. (I've learned this lesson the hard way).

Regardless of whether you are working with a buyer or with a seller, your ideal working day should be eight hours, five days a week, with six weeks off in a calendar year. However, when you begin your real estate endeavour, it is more likely to be 16 to 18 hours, seven days a week, 365 days a year. (Guilty as charged.)

I keep hearing people who are starting a new business saying: "I must work that much. I am just starting my business." Wrong again. No need to do that, but if you don't have the systems in place, and/or you don't have someone like me to share this valuable information with you, you will be working those harsh hours and will be draining the life out of your eyes, unnecessarily.

So, let me give you some of those hours back, that you can use for your vacation days.

VACATION DAYS SAVING SYSTEM – BUYERS

1. 4 W'S prequalification
2. Mortgage pre-approval in written form
3. Deposit/down payment proof
4. Must, Nice and "not in this life" checklist

VACATION DAYS SAVING SYSTEM – SELLERS

1. 4 W'S prequalification
2. Mortgage outstanding balance on the selling property (is there enough money to pay off all the debt attached to the property (mortgages, liens etc), and to have enough money for agent commissions?)
3. Mortgage pre-approval in written form –
   (if purchasing at the same time)
4. Must, Nice and "not in this life" checklist –
   (if purchasing at the same time)

CHAPTER 8

UNDERSTANDING BUYERS' & SELLERS' NEEDS & WANTS

In the previous chapter, I gave you some technical tips on how to make your life as a realtor a bit easier when dealing with buyers and sellers.

Now, let's do some work on how, by helping your clients, you can make your life as a realtor even easier and more pleasant. The end result is you will not be tired and frustrated, and your clients will love you so much that referrals will keep pouring in. All that by caring a bit more for your clients than anyone else does.

My eye opener, as a salesperson, was the book *Kiss, Bow or Shake Hands* by Terri Morrison and Wayne A. Conaway. In this book you will find international business etiquette on how to do business in more then 60 countries in the world.

After I read that book, I realized there is absolutely no culture that I've done business with before that I didn't offend, in one way or another. Unintentionally and without being aware of it, of course!

I was born and raised in a country that was closed, and unique in many ways. Because it was closed, I was not exposed to other cultures of the world. Before I came to Canada in 1999, I'd never seen, or communicated in person with, someone who spoke a different language, had different skin colour or practised a different religion (except from seeing them in movies, on TV or in movie theaters).

My lack of knowledge and understanding of different cultures made me very curious to learn more about them. I've read many books, watched documentaries, spoken with my new friends and clients, and genuinely did my best to learn as much and as fast as I could, for two reasons. Firstly, to stop offending people! And secondly, to help me understand how to do business better with them.

For someone coming from such a "mono-cultured" country, I surely have had clients from almost every continent in the world!

Keep listening and learn as much as you can about different cultures – about how they do business, how they live their lives, how they celebrate and everything else.

BUYERS' NEEDS & WANTS

Living in Canada and being a part of a multicultural country is amazing and yet it can be a challenge when working in that environment if you are not aware of a different culture's traditions and expectations.

I had clients from Malaysia and I showed them many houses. Even though the houses were all in their price range, and had all the features they wanted, they kept declining to move forward with an offer on any of the houses we'd seen. I was truly puzzled and kept referring them back to their wants and needs. And yet still the answer was no. We did that dance for some time, until I got the nerve to actually ask "what the heck is going on here?" (In nicer words, of course.)

Finally, they opened up to me. They believed and lived their life by following the "feng shui" system and were shy to tell me that, thinking I would not agree with them. "Who am I to agree with anything?" I said. "I am here merely to follow your lawful instructions." They explained what feng shui considers good and bad in a property. I made a list of those items, and since then, whenever I was selecting properties for them, I referred back to that list. TA-DA... saved us so much time... After that, I signed up for a few feng shui courses, read as many articles as I could and kept learning about it throughout the years. As my dear friend Chery says -" I don't care much about it", which is polite way of saying, I personally don't give a damn about it, but I still made an effort to learn and understand it, for the benefit of my clients, for the benefit of saving time, and for the benefit of my own sanity...:)

Now, since I have learned from that previous "cultural clash," the next time I met with a client for our initial appointment, I would ask. "Aside from your 'wants and nice-to-have list,' is there something else that I should pay attention to? Is there something that is not aligning with your culture that is very important to you that I should look for?"

You could sense the huge load falling off the client's shoulders when I ask that. Eureka!

If you would like to have another gas-spending/head-turning/life-learning lesson, please make sure you ask as many questions as possible, before you even get into the car.

But, wait, there's more! Like those TV commercials say: Buy one and get a few free items, for the same price!

We've covered cultural requirements, now let's have some more fun – at my expense, of course – with other potential problems with properties.

Another family was buying their first home in Canada. Homebuying educational session done, new cultural questions added and asked, and off we go for some house shopping with my awesome buyers. Some houses were somewhat good, some of them were missing something, some of them were perfect, but the answer was still "no offer for this one." Several weeks of showings passed, no offers for them yet, and I remembered that one of the houses seemed to have all they needed, but they had discarded that one too.

Since I am a smart-ass now, I asked bluntly, "What was wrong with that house we saw last week?" The husband said, "Did you see the hideous red colour walls in that bedroom?" My famous "donkey ears" started growing on my head, and I could even hear the "hee-haw" loud

and clear. (What are my "donkey ears" you ask?
Where I am from in Europe it was a term used
to mean you just realized a stupid mistake you
made!) Ooook, I said. The paint for that room is
a few hundred dollars. Was the room size OK? He
said "yes." Was the house otherwise OK for you?
He said, "yes, it is perfect. We love everything
else."

Good. If that room was painted in the colour
you prefer, would you be interested in placing an
offer on that home? Absolutely, he said. A few
days later, we made an offer, with a clause asking
for that bedroom to be painted white. Deal done,
clients happy, new question added to my growing
questionnaire list.

I was happy with my new list. I believed I'd covered
everything. Until I met my next buyers.

Have you noticed how most of the stories are about the
buyers? Yeah, because with sellers you will have the same
questions and objections over and over, so not many surprises
there. But we will cover those too, later in this chapter. Now,
let's go back to laughing at my hiccups.

I'd met my new clients at my open house. A lovely couple.
They didn't like the house I had an open house for, so I offered
them my services and we scheduled our buyers' educational
session. All checked out, ALL questions asked and answered,
and we started our search. For these clients, I had to pay
attention to the south-facing homes and I was so proud of
myself, how great I was at selecting the listings to show them.

We spent some time searching for a home for them. At one house, I rang the bell, opened the door for a three-level townhouse and let my clients in. The wife went in first and, as she started climbing the stairs, she turned back, very pale in the face and almost fainting. Her husband just got her under his arms and they went outside. I looked up and saw a few cats on the stairs and one on a banister. It turned out the wife was extremely scared of cats, though not allergic (thank God!). We left that place and since then, another question about animal issues and allergies is added to my questionnaire list. AND I make sure to always be the first one entering the house.

So, to wrap up, since your stomach probably hurts from laughing at my expense, here are some questions you should ask your clients, before you go out for showings:

1. Is feng shui part of your everyday life?
2. Any specific cultural requirements in regard to the property position?
3. Any allergies on pets/carpets etc.?
4. Any issues with house numbers, closeness to the hospitals, cemeteries, highways etc.?
5. ANY OTHER RESTRICTIONS I SHOULD KNOW ABOUT?

These are just some of the important questions that will help you understand your clients better and will save them and you plenty of time and effort. If you eliminate these potential issues, you and your clients will be able to focus more on the homes themselves. That should result in a better experience for them, since they won't feel bad for loving the house and hating the position of it – or whatever the issue may be.

I am sure there are way more questions you can add to make your clients' homebuying experience much better and hiccup-free. They will love you for that, and when they hear someone complaining about their experience with their realtor, I am sure they will point out how great and caring you were, and they will very likely send them your way.

You will get so much by doing so little. All it takes is to ask questions and listen to what's important to them. If they want a house in a specific school boundary, don't waste your time and theirs by showing them a "perfect home" in a different school district. One of my recent clients was an amazing young gentleman who is very environmentally conscious, loves to eat healthy and cooks and bakes his own food. Can you guess what was one of his requirements under a "must" list? BULK BARN! For those of you who don't know what that is, it is a store that sells specialty foods by bulk. There is vegan, gluten-free, non-GMO, baking supplies and some not-so-healthy food too, like my favourite sour gummy candies. Searching for a first home for him was a breeze, thanks to my five "must/nice/no way" list. We had clearly laid out requirements and there were no issues or misunderstanding in regard to boundaries.

Always refer back to the "must, nice and don't" list. Check their five must-haves, five nice-to-have and five don't-show-these-homes-to-me list. If they send you a house that doesn't match their original criteria, refer back to the list and ask if you should adjust the list, so you can stay on track. Sometimes, the buyers get carried away, sometimes they really don't know what their number one priority is, and most of the time they will need to adjust their criteria, during the homebuying process. I have yet to meet a client who bought what they say they want, during our initial meeting, for the price they say they want, in the location they say they want. And that is absolutely normal.

The buyer, unless they are in the business themselves, usually has high expectations, due to all the false advertising online and TV. They see a great house for a ridiculous price and they want it. What they don't see is that the listing was active, sold or not, five years ago. It is sitting on realtor's websites (often not removed) and that can create unrealistic expectations.

That is why it is very important to have some kind of questionnaire to send to the client before the scheduled educational session. That way, you can see what they are expecting and you can get ready to bring them back to reality (if needed) and handle their objections with ease. Also, you will need to educate them that very likely, during their home search, they will need to revise their criteria. Either they will need to adjust their expectations or their budget. It sounds cruel, but it is not. You will be doing them a great favour, by keeping it clear and realistic.

They might not like it at the beginning, but they will understand, once they start the process and, hopefully, respect you for that at the end of the transaction.

SELLERS' NEEDS & WANTS

What are the sellers' expectations? They want to achieve the best terms, in the shortest amount of time, for the least expense, of course. I know, my eyes are rolling too, but it is what it is. I don't see it as a negative, but rather a positive. As opposed to the buyers, when not even they know what they really want, with sellers it's a clear picture. You know most of their objections, so get ready to address them and the experience will be good for all sides.

In the previous few pages, I kept suggesting that every realtor should have some kind of questionnaire to send to the buyers, before they first meet, so you can understand what it is that they want and what are their expectations and objections.

Absolutely the same applies to sellers.

Create a form where you ask them the usual questions about the house, property tax, improvements, will they be buying and selling at the same time, but add something like this too: "What do you love the most about your home?" "If you could change anything in your home, what would it be?" "What are you not fond of in your current home?" And sneak in a few questions that will paint a better picture for you, in regard to what to expect as their objections when you show up for that listing presentation.

"What is the expected listing price?" and "How much do you expect to net out from this sale?" seem to be the best ones, to find out if they are aligned with the market and how much they know about it. If they give you a number that is close to the market value, that will show you that they know the market and you will need to give them information that they don't have. Remember, you need to prove to them that you know more than they do and that they NEED you.

You will need to sharpen your knowledge about that specific neighbourhood and/or property, and find some information they are not likely to know.

Once you point that out, hopefully it will gain you some brownie points and you will be seen as "someone who knows their job".

You will need to refer back to the book *Kiss, Bow or Shake Hands* to make sure you are addressing the sellers in a way they would more likely go along with. Remember, different cultures do business differently. Do proper research before your listing appointment. Try to get as much information as you can about the sellers and their experience with their current home. Are any of the owners emotionally tied to the property? How can you make them feel better and less stressed out during the sale? Do they need to see the theatrics of negotiation? If yes, you will need to know how to explain the true value of the property, and how the listing price tag is not to be construed as a value.

If you learn what drives certain cultures to agree to certain terms, you will more likely land that listing and it will likely be a very pleasant experience for all parties involved in this transaction.

As you can see, it is not just giving me the property address, number of bedrooms and bathrooms and I will send you a CMA (comparative market analysis). You can do that, of course, but then you will be just like the other few realtors they've spoken with, so why should they choose you?

But if you start asking them questions and genuinely show more interest in their story, you will be "different" and they will look at you more favourably and more likely be open to your suggestions regarding the listing work that should be done and/or the service fee charged.

Now you've done all your homework and off you go for that listing appointment. Show up five minutes early. We all know that sales representative's mantra: "If you are early, you are on time, if you are on time, you are late, if you are late, you are forgotten." Be professional, dress appropriately (please don't show up in shorts and flip flops, and yes, I've seen that too), and use proper language. They are not yet your friends. Even more so, if they are.

Remember what happened to me and my friends who knew me for many years and the comment I got from them? Don't repeat my mistake.

Back to your presentation today. Let's play some more mind games. Once you're inside the house, try to sit at the kitchen table (such a cliché, I know, but there is a reason for it). People are usually most comfy on a couch in a living room, but you don't want them to be comfy and zone out, you want them focused. The kitchen is a safe place for them, since that is where they share their food with their family and friends, and that subconsciously places you as their "maybe-friend" too.

Don't sit at the head of the table in case the seller has a huge ego but sit at a prominent place so they will know you are running the show. Make sure to invite them (if they are a couple) to sit next to you – one on each side. If one of the sellers is "busy doing something," politely tell them that you will gladly wait for them to join you. Do NOT do a listing presentation to only one seller. (did that mistake stupidly too). You might actually miss the decision maker and all your work and hours of preparation would be in vain. As a matter of fact, you should point out to them, during the initial call, that both of them are expected to be present during the whole presentation.

Now, that you are all sitting at the table and you have your computer up and running, you can start the meeting.

Lets see what are the sellers' usual questions:

- ☺ Why should I list my house with you?
- ☺ How many sales did you have this year?
- ☺ Is this the area you work in?
- ☺ Where will you advertise the listing?
- ☺ Are you going to stage it?
- ☺ How much do you charge? (Although they want to, and most of the time they do, ask this question first.)

For most of the questions, I am sure you have a great response in place already. If you are a new agent, you were probably told this already: Use your office sales numbers. I will focus on the one question that we all have been, or are still struggling with. The scary one: "What is your commission?" I hate those words so much that during my consultation with sellers and buyers, I refer to it as a "service fee."

My first tip for you is to leave the answer to the service fee question as the last question to address. If that is their first question, just politely tell them you will address that one in detail at the end of the presentation. Show them what you will do for them, how different you are from the other agents, and then give them a few options to choose from regarding the service fee. People like to feel as if they have a choice, and are not being given one option only. However, structure your service fee setup in a way that they must choose the "best" option (to which you will lead them softly, of course).

Here is how I do it: My listing presentation has a complete breakdown table of all services I provide, in order to sell a property, for the best terms and in the shortest amount of time. There are four pages of listed items that show I will NOT just take pictures and list it on a local real estate board, but will do so much more. A few of the top items listed still are "I will upload your home listing on MLS (Multiple Listing Service) and Realtor.ca."

Are you rolling your eyes again? Well, don't. I've heard a story of a fellow realtor who did an awesome listing presentation. He showed them how he will pay for staging, have pictures done by a great photographer, a virtual tour with many options, advertise it in foreign countries and so much more, but they chose to list their home up for sale with another agent. He was really surprised and asked them how come they chose that agent over him. Their answer was: "He said that he will put it on MLS, and you didn't offer that in your presentation." I guess I am not the only one who gets those "donkey ears" from time to time, am I?

Do not assume anything. Whatever is common sense to you, is not necessarily even "ever heard of" by the other side.

I am sure you will own quite a few of those "ears" in your career too, because if you don't, that means you didn't work at all. But try to learn from someone else's mistakes, and minimize your own pain in the rear.

> *A few years back, I had a one-on-one meeting with a fellow BNI member (Business Networking International). In those private meetings, we are trying to understand each other's businesses as much as we can, so we can do our best to refer business to each other. She was asking me the usual questions about the procedure of selling a house. I was explaining to her about the process of sales transaction money disbursements, and without paying too much attention, I slid in the words "after the seller pays both agents." Her eyes opened wide and she said surprisingly: "What do you mean, the seller pays both agents?" Now my eyes got wide open too. My mind was like "whaaaat? She doesn't know that the seller pays both agents? That is 'common sense.'"*

Well, it is not. Unless you are in the business, the lingo and the rules are not common for all to know. For those of you who know me, you know that if you start speaking in "technical" language, I will stop you and say "plain English, please!" Believe me, people like to listen to "plain English" but will not necessarily ask you to speak that way.

Lesson learned, and now I make sure that both sides, buyers and sellers, are informed who pays what, during our initial appointment, regardless of which side they are on. There is not a week that goes by that I don't recall the saying "We keep learning all our lives, and we will still die stupid."

To go back to my listing presentation service fee template: I have three options to choose from, but you can have as many options as you like. There is no right or wrong way here. My service fee table has checkmark boxes and it is very easy for sellers to distinguish the difference. A little "brain trick" I've used while creating this form is that i named those options, not just by percentage, (2.5%, 2% etc.), but rather with the words: "LIMITED," "SMART" and "PLATINUM" plans, with percentage written in much smaller size underneath. Which option would you choose?

The "Smart" plan, I assume, (since we all want to look and be smart). So, that is the one I use, as an option that I prefer to charge. "Platinum" would cost more than an average commission fee, but will have some extra luxury point services that I sometimes add as "freebies" if they select a "Smart" plan. The "Limited" option would be customized all the time, depending on who I am dealing with and how much I am willing to lower my commission for that client, in case they really don't want, or can't afford, to pay my full service fee.

There will be some of the more expensive services, which I usually cover for, cut in that plan. Most of the time, people would like to choose and be the "Smart" ones. But if they can't afford it, and I really like them, I will customize a brand-new plan for them, out of those three.

If I prefer not to work with them, I will be firm on my already offered services. That way, I have a way out, without looking like an a** in their eyes.

Does it work all the time? No, but if I try everything I can to show the client that I will provide an outstanding service and that the expense is well justified, and they are still being stubborn on what they want to pay, then it will be absolutely my choice if I will take them as my clients or not.

Be proud and respect yourself and your worth, and the stars will align your way.

Unless they are self-centered egomaniacs, after presenting in detail how you will help them maximize the outcome of selling their property, for the best terms and in the shortest time possible, it is extremely likely they will choose and trust you.

Will you take the listing if they don't agree to all your terms? Just know it is your choice, not theirs. Often agents say, "I didn't have a choice, and I had to take a discounted rate for my services." What BS! You always have a choice. I am not saying that it will be a good or bad choice, I am simply saying that you DO have a choice.

They have the right to refuse to pay you a full service fee, but if you do the best to find a middle ground and there is still no agreement, then you have the right to decide if you would like to work with them or not. If you don't value your expertise and time, why should they? Sellers can smell the desperation of "commission breath," so be aware how you present yourselves.

If you are desperate to make the deal, they will feel it, and they will win the negotiating game against you. Those clients will be a nightmare to work with, since they will have a sense that they are better than you. They will likely be complaining about everything, giving you instructions on how to do your job, and won't be satisfied at the end, after all your hard work.

To clarify, I am not talking about your friends, family or past clients, that you may voluntarily give a discount. I am merely speaking about those who see you for the first time in your life.

To wrap up this portion of what sellers need and want, make sure you get the most information before you go to the appointment. Not just about the house, but about their family too. Listen carefully. Maybe you will hear a dog barking, or children talking while on the phone/zoom with them. Use that to build a rapport when you arrive. Bring a pet toy, and/or a children's colouring book, or toy, depending on the kids age, when you arrive for a listing presentation. I am sure that the sellers will be pleasantly surprised, it will keep the kids occupied and you should have the sellers undivided attention. It will keep them occupied and you will have the parents focus more on you. Please avoid bringing any kind of food, since you don't know people's food regimens and styles and you really don't want to piss off the parents by bringing candies to their kids if they never give them sugar.

The more prepared you are, the more likely it is for you to get that listing. As a matter of fact, I am the one suggesting sellers interview a few agents, when they first contact me, if they haven't scheduled that already. The only favour I ask of them is to let me present last. That way, they have someone to compare me with.

Don't be afraid.

If you practise your script well and do your homework diligently, you WILL stand above the crowd. Most of these exact tips I am giving you are available somewhere in the world of the internet today, and yet so very few have ever implemented them.

WORKING WITH BUYERS AND SELLERS PROS AND CONS

Working with people is a time-consuming, nerve-racking rollercoaster, but we still do it. And some of us actually love working with people. What is wrong with us? Seriously!

Let me show you some pros and cons of working with different types of clients. This is not 100% accurate with each and every one of them, but can give you a picture of what potentially to expect when working with them.

WORKING WITH BUYERS

PROS:

- ☺ They usually get to know you/trust you faster than sellers, since you will be spending more time with them.
- ☺ You might get a chance to meet their family members, who potentially could become your clients (happens often).

- Not as many expenses as if you are on the listing side.
- Buyers usually don't negotiate your commission.

CONS:

- Time-consuming and limits you to working with only one person at a time.
- Money spent on gas shouldn't be too bad (unless you are as dumb as I was at the beginning of my career, and worked with non-qualified buyers). Your serving area should be within a 30-minute drive of your home. But if you live in GTA (Greater Toronto Area) and or any other megacity, that will easily be an hour or so).
- Reaching the point of an actual accepted offer might be a lengthy process, depending on how determined and rushed they are to purchase.
- Their criteria and qualifications can change in the middle of the process.
- Those same parents and relatives who can be your best allies and potential clients, can (read "will") likely be your worst enemies too. They will complain and argue about almost anything and everything. (I actually had a buyer backing away from a deal on my listing because his parents came to see the house and realized the exposure of the front door is not on a favourable side.)

However, even with all these cons, being on the buyers side and seeing their rollercoaster of emotions can be rewarding – from excited faces when we make the offer, to their scared faces the next day, to the happy tears once they get the keys and bring their families to their new home. As I always tell them, "you might forget my name in 10 or 20 years, but you will never forget that there was one lady who helped you when we were searching for your first home." You cherish those moments forever.

Can you determine who are my favourite clients now?

Yes, first-time homebuyers are my favourite people, and if they are new immigrants I love them even more. I can assure you that most other agents would roll their eyes and send me to hell right now.

I am a first generation of immigrants here in Canada and I can completely understand their concerns and questions, and when I start addressing them, before they even have the courage to ask them, I can see their eyes lit with the light and hope. THAT is my drive, my fuel.

Now, this doesn't mean YOU have to work with first-time homebuyers. Honestly, they are the toughest cookies you can get. So, I suggest you do a little soul searching, and YOU decide who will be your perfect client.

Each group will have its own pros and cons and each one of them is unique, in its own way.

WORKING WITH SELLERS

PROS:
- Usually a faster process
- Not much driving involved (unless you list a house far from your location)

- ⊚ Your sign and online marketing might bring you more leads
- ⊚ You can work with multiple clients at the same time since you are not physically tied with sellers every day, once the listing is up.
- ⊚ Somewhat less emotion involved, unless they are downsizing, or it was their first home that they are selling. (Listen and try to find a solution on how to help them, to make it less painful)

CONS:

- ⊚ Can be very expensive – staging, virtual tours, advertising, painting etc., depending on what you offer your client in your fee plan
- ⊚ Very likely they will try to negotiate your fee down.
- ⊚ There is no guarantee that the property will sell and you might get burned for the expense, unless you have and implement a retainer plan.

Working with sellers is an art on its own. Are they buying at the same time too? Should you list first, or should you help them buy first? You will have some work to do there.

You will need to figure out what is most important to them and prepare a plan based on that.

So, if they will sell their property ONLY if they find a property in their desired school boundary area, then you will definitely need to work on buying the new home first. But you will need to show them all potential hiccups if they decide to take that route. They will need to make sure that their finances are in order and that they won't suffer too much in case their home doesn't sell and they need to carry both mortgages and other expenses for some time, or if the closing dates are not matching. They will need to involve the mortgage specialist, accountant and potentially even a lawyer, before they make ANY decision. Be careful of what you advise! If you are not sure, double check with your broker of record, office manager or a senior agent you can trust.

WHICH ONES SHOULD YOU WORK WITH, BUYERS OR SELLERS?

There is no correct answer to this question. You will need to find what works best for you.

Many of the best-known coaches in the world say you should focus on sellers only. I can't say I agree much with that statement though, in today's market. They also say beginners usually focus on buyers, since it is easier to convince someone to buy with you than to sell, and new agents usually don't have much money to invest in listings (advertising, staging, photography, floor plans and all the rest). Which could be wrong again.

Some coaches will say you should be at a 50/50 ratio, between buyers and sellers, some will say that if you want to be a "successful" agent, you should have an 80/20 ratio, in favour of the seller. Again, BS!

Before the internet became a crucial part of our everyday living, I would agree with that statement. You would need a listing to put up your sign on the lawn so people can see your name out there to contact you, and that way you would generate more business. It seemed more feasible, as opposed to if you didn't have any listings to advertise in the newspaper.

However, today, in a world where information is at the tip of your fingers, as long as you have access to the internet, you can work mainly with buyers and still be very successful.

I will repeat it again, there is no "right" or "wrong" way of who you should be working with. Whatever you sincerely believe will work best for you, and that you truly enjoy doing, will work for you and will make you one of the successful agents for sure.

Working with buyers can be very pleasant. You are seeing them more often, you are meeting with their children and family members, they share their life stories and usually become closer to you, than if you are working with a seller. Maybe that time-consuming con we mentioned earlier in the book actually is not a con, but a pro? By spending so much time with them and their family, they get to know you, like you, trust you, and as a final result of that, to send more clients your way. You didn't need to spend thousands of dollars on cold lead-generating systems. Those clients are already halfway vetted, (as long as you actually did an outstanding job, of course) and your business will grow substantially.

As long as you nurture relationships with your clients, your success as a real estate agent is almost guaranteed, regardless of the silly sellers/buyers ratio.

If you are not keen on all this legwork, maybe you can focus on sellers more.

Working with sellers has its own perks too.

The shorter time spent with sellers can be an opportunity to prospect for more clients, and it seems a better use of your time. Again, nothing wrong with it. You are the only one who can tell what works best for you.

The way I see it, the biggest advantage of working with sellers is that with listings, you are promoting yourself. It is your marketing platform, showing people that you are a working real estate agent and not a "secret agent," and the bonus is that you get your pretty face on their lawn too. Just recently, I listed a house close to my friend's house. It happened fast and I didn't have time to tell her I would be listing a house up for sale in her neighbourhood. After an hour of having a sign installed on the lawn, sure enough, my friend called me. She said: "Matilda, I was just walking the dogs and saw a sign from far. I thought, oh, that girl looks like Matilda. Wait, that IS Matilda."

A few other friends drive home every day through that street, so some personal advertising was present. Guess who's name was mentioned at our community party that weekend?... there was some free advertising for me. Regardless if they liked me or not, they had mentioned my name.... My sign on the lawn was screaming "in your face, people! I am a rockstar real estate agent!"

Imagine your friends speaking about you to someone they know and then that person sees your sign on a lawn. That would be another confirmation, to that positive introduction that your friend did for you.

So the perfect solution, in my opinion, is to have a nice mix of both buyers and sellers, with the scale tipping over slightly to the side you prefer to work with.

CHAPTER 9

CLIENT PREQUALIFICATIONS THE FINANCIAL PART

Before you get too excited and start driving clients around to show houses, please make sure you finish the complete pre-qualifying process. You've got their needs and wants, you made sure they are not just tire kickers. But did you clarify the financial part too? Do they even qualify to buy a property? Do they have money for a deposit and down payment? Is there really equity in their current home that they can rely on to buy a new home? Is the money theirs, or borrowed? We need to do some more homework before you go out.

MORTGAGE PRE-APPROVAL IN WRITTEN FORM

In my first year in business here in Canada, I learned a "tire kicker" lesson, and I learned it painfully. A young couple contacted me from my ad in a newspaper and asked to see the house I was advertising. We went there and they didn't like it. I'd offered them my help and, of course, I did the 4 W's questions. They lived in a rental and wanted their own place, AND they both worked.

But what I didn't ask is if they had a mortgage pre-approval. To summarize: After six months of showings all over the GTA, we drove hundreds of kilometers together, not to mention how much that was in gas money, and we found a place. The next day I received a call from them saying they went to the bank and they could not qualify for a mortgage, since they had declared bankruptcy a few years back. What a bummer. I literally felt donkey ears growing on my head!

The good thing from this saga was that I've learned the GTA marketplace, like nobody else. I now know every little town, every little street, road, dead end and all different types of houses.

Well, lesson learned. Since then, at the time I do a buyers' presentation with clients, I specify that we will not be going out to see any properties until we have something in writing from a lending institution. I prefer that to be someone from the list I have, know and trust. But I don't mind if they have their own mortgage specialist, as long as I receive something in writing showing how much they qualify for.

I am sure some people would disagree with this, saying that is their own private matter. But if you are their agent, you owe them a fiduciary duty, which means you owe them accountability and confidentiality too. Therefore, there is no reason for them not to disclose this information to you.

TIP 1:

Always ask for a mortgage pre-approval.

When you are a new agent, or you've been "dry" for months, you tend to rush things. Being scared that they will go to someone else, makes it even worse and you might rush into taking them to show them houses, hoping they will stick with you. My two cents for you are: If they are "tire kickers," let them go and not burn you. Wouldn't you rather be home with your family, or just watching TV, instead of driving around for a long time, spending time and money, just to realize that you will not get paid at all?

TIP 2:

Very often, most real estate offices and real estate boards will have someone from bank institutions doing seminars with information about new mortgage products, new rules and so on. Make sure you attend as many of them as possible, regardless of whether you are a new agent or not. Get to know a few mortgage specialists from regular banks and mono-lenders as well, and keep learning. The more you know about mortgages, the easier it will be for you to advise your clients.

I am not saying you need to become a mortgage broker, but if you know what institutions are looking for when pre-qualifying clients, you will know from day one if yours are qualified buyers and you can guide them in the right direction. Maybe they can't qualify at the moment, but you can create a team with a mortgage specialist and make a plan for them, and you can help the buyers achieve their goals safely and hiccup free.

Most people genuinely do not know if they can qualify or not. They make good salaries, but they might have bruised credit, or no down payment money. Maybe they came to the country a few months back and they don't have a credit history. Maybe they want to move to a larger house, but there's not enough equity in the current one to sell. There are so many scenarios, and you can't predict what the potential issues would be. Hence, get to know a great mortgage broker and team up with them.

A few years back, a very good client of mine referred me to their friend who was new to the country. After my initial conversation with him, I realized that even though he had started a great job and had some money for a down payment, he was here on a work permit visa and had just applied for permanent resident status. Since he had just applied that month, I knew the process would last a few years for sure, so I added him to my "C list." But I did not just drop his name there.

I connected him with a great mortgage specialist and together we created a great plan for him. The mortgage specialist was working on building up his credit history, by advising him which and how many credit cards to open, how to use them and more. At the same time, I'd taken time to educate him on different neighbourhoods, different types of properties. We went out to browse some properties and neighbourhoods together, and we came to a conclusion on which one would be the best choice for him. By the time he received a letter confirming his permanent resident status, we were fully ready to execute the home shopping process. Within a few weeks from receiving his permanent resident letter, we had already selected, negotiated and bought a wonderful property for him.

The whole process took around 18 months, but the painless and fun-filled buying process was done within a few weeks. The client was very happy, there were no headaches or heartbreaks and everyone was happy at the end. Needless to say, I've gained a great, loyal client and a friend, and more referrals came from him too.

Remember: You are here to stay. You have to be patient, but ready to act fast, if needed. Don't look for instant gratification only. Otherwise, you will not last long in this business. Plant a seed and watch it grow.

This approach can land you countless loyal clients, who will send you more business regularly.

DEPOSIT AND DOWN PAYMENT PROOF

A deposit is very important and often people are not aware how soon they will need it. And what's even worse, they are not sure how easily they can release the money from their bank account.

Just recently, I had a nice house listed up for sale, and when I called one of the agents who showed the property to ask for feedback, he said his client loved the house, but they told him now they don't have deposit funds for it. I was about to ask why he hates himself! He wasted his time showing this house, and God knows how many other houses too. He wasted the time of his clients too, since they are obviously not aware of the process, and not qualified to buy. And in the end, he wasted my clients' time too. They had to clean and prepare the house to be presentable for showing, while managing two very young children at the same time.

TIP 1:

Make sure you educate your client on the difference between the deposit and down payment, and when each of those monies is needed by. Ask your buyers, before you go out for showings, where the deposit and down payment are coming from. The funds must be available for closing day, so your next question is "is your money in any type of savings account, including an RRSP" and/or if the money is coming in from another country? All banks have different rules about how long money has to be in the account.

I had a buyer who contacted me out of the blue and wanted to make an offer on a house. Luckily, I asked him where the down payment was coming from and he said that he will use his RRSP. I said, Oh you have money there? He was so excited to tell me that "a friend" told him that he should put money into RRSP, so he pays less income tax, and he can use it for a down payment, as a first-time homebuyer. Great, I said. When did you put the money in?, I asked. "Last week" he said. An alarm in my head went off. "Did you know that the money must be in the account for a minimum of three months, before you can actually use it, unless you want it to be fully taxed? I asked. "No," he answered. "My friend didn't tell me that." Is your friend an accountant? I added. You very likely know his answer by now. "No," he said.

Well, in that case, we will need to let this house go, since they need a 30-day closing, and we can continue to search for houses that will have closing that would accommodate the timing of your RRSP withdrawal. He was heartbroken, since he really liked the house.

You do not need to be an accountant, or to know all this information, but my advice to you is to make sure you know where the money is coming from, and for them to confirm with their mortgage providers and accountants that they have cleared money for the deposit and down payment. This way, you will save yourself and your clients unnecessary headaches.

Another thing you should be aware of is that it's not only buyers that should be pre-qualified. You should do the same for the sellers as well, regardless of whether they will be buying and selling, or just selling.

Let's say someone calls you to list their property. You get excited, you do everything by the book and smoothly get the house sold. Then, just before closing, you receive a "not so nice" call from your deal department and/or lawyer, saying there is no money for the agents' commission. Are your eyebrows up to the top of your head yet? No? OK, let's speed up that process for you.

You DID check the land registry and they bought the house a long time ago, and you DID sell the house much more than purchase price in the past. So, technically, there is enough equity for all commissions and leftovers too, right? Wrong. Did you check if they had a few more mortgages registered on the title? And if you've listened to the law course you had in real estate college, you should know the order of how the money is distributed after the sale. If you didn't, it's OK, I'll enlighten you: The agent's commission is at the bottom of the list. If there is any money left, you will be paid, of course.

Just recently I had a deal not close due to Seller's default. The listing agent did check the land registry before listing it up for sale, and according to the amount of the mortgages (yes, there was more then one mortgage registered on the title), selling price was enough to cover the mortgages and all lawyer's and agent's expenses. However, what apparently not even the seller was aware of was that the last mortgage on title was a private mortgage, and because he was breaking up the mortgage sooner, his penalties were over $22,000. The seller couldn't find that money and since buyer couldn't get a clear and mortgage free title, the deal was cancelled. You can't even imagine the stress and pain the buyers went through.

This is one of the reason that I stopped congratulating clients when they firm up on a deal. I just say "we are one step closer, but the home will be yours once you get the keys".

I might be over-cautious, but clients do appreciate the truth.

TIP 2:

Make sure you ask the probing question about the finances before you sign a contract. Make a checklist and send it to them before visiting for the final signing documents session.

The checklist should have the usual: property tax amount, any rentals, any updates on the property, but also slide in, how many mortgages are registered against the property, how many line of credits are registered against the property, what is the total mortgage(s) and/or line of credit(s) balance on it ... and if they are aware of any potential penalties in case they break the mortgage terms.

TIP 3:

If they are selling and buying at the same time, make sure they got in writing a pre-approval and triple check with the lender if they are qualified for a bridge loan, if needed.

CHAPTER 10

A DAY IN THE LIFE
OF A REALTOR

You have checked everything, you have all your ducks in a row, so now you can finally get into that fancy car of yours, and start showing houses, or do the listing presentation.

I would like to dedicate this chapter to all those realtors out there who have no idea of what common sense means. And unfortunately, there are too many of those out there.

Even if you DO have common sense, please read this one carefully. There will be some good tips for buyers and listing agents for sure.

SHOWING FUN TIMES

This topic should not EVER be a part of any book, IF people had common sense, were respectful and decent. You might see this as an insult, but please don't. We've all heard a great deal of bad stories going around. Even if you had only one listing in your career, I am sure you had sellers calling you saying how agents didn't show up. Or maybe they showed up five hours late, or used a washroom without flushing the toilet, (unfortunately I saw that one quite a few times) left the doors unlocked and even wide open, and the list goes on.

So, therefore, I will go through the common courtesy tips for home showings, for both listing agents and buyer's agents.

When having a listing, your goal is to sell the property in the shortest amount of time, for the best terms possible. I will not talk about the staging, photography and other details, since I am sure you've done that properly already. Right?!
What I would like to talk about are showings. I find that portion of the process to be the most neglected one.

Let's hope you have all the lights on in the house for showings, but did you tell your sellers to make sure the house has a pleasant room temperature? If it is summer and you walk into a freezer of a house, that might not be pleasant for some people and they might run out of it too soon. The end result is a lost potentially perfect buyer. The same will apply if it is winter and your house is like a freezer again.

How is the smell in the house? Minimizing cooking spices is advisable during the selling time, or as I always like to tell the sellers: "Until the house is sold, it's pasta season."

Here are some more important tips that people neglect to advise clients of. And most of us had NO fun witnessing them:

- ☺ Have your porch light ON at night! Who knows how many times we had to do a scavenger hunt for a lockbox in a pitch-dark night.
- ☺ Make sure the driveway and walkway toward the

house are clear of snow and ice in the winter. (I've witnessed a few funny, but not-so-funny falls.)

☺ Make sure the lockbox is COVERED and protected from weather elements! I've had to drive to a hardware store to buy lock de-icer and then drive back so I could unfreeze the lockbox that was covered in snow. (I carry a small bottle of it in my car now.)

☺ Have all drapes open on the windows, even if the view is not good. It is better for the buyer to see it right away rather than walk away from the deal once they see it during the inspection.

☺ Remove all animals from the property for all showings. Too many times we had to pass on the perfect house for my buyers because they wouldn't enter the house due to being scared of the animals. I was surprised how many people were afraid of cats! (I'm not even gonna talk about a house I visited many years ago in Mississauga that had a big red snake, a chameleon, a cage filled with rats, two huge dogs and a cat in it!)

☺ Please ask them to leave the house in a nice condition and not to have clothes all over the house. (Yes, I did see a pair of dirty male underwear on the floor! I still gag when I remember that condo.)

☺ Advise them NOT to be in the house! (My client opened the bathroom door and a seller was just getting out for the shower! How embarrassing! He damn well knew we were coming! Now that I think of it, maybe he did it BECAUSE he knew we were coming? Yack!)

☺ Ask them to remove valuables and prescribed medication from the property, or to hide them somewhere. It is for everyone's good.

There are many more tips, but I will leave some of them for you to discover and record.

Now, let's talk about every day's work as a buyers' agent:

You get up, turn on the computer and start searching for properties for your client. How do you choose the order of listings you show to your client? Do you start with the one you think they will like the least, and then move up toward the one they might like the best, or show them the best house first and work backwards?

Well, there is no rule. The order should be different, depending on your client. You have to know them!

If they are the type that is slow in making decisions, then it might be a good idea to leave the best for last. But if they are a quick decision maker, then maybe show them the best one first and once they see the next few, it will be easier for them to make a decision on the spot. The one thing you can't do is to rush them into making a decision.

There is no rule on how many houses a person should see before making a decision. Some will make a decision after seeing three houses and some will need to see 30 or more. Yeah, those might be tough cookies to close, but the most important thing is that they need to be comfortable with their decision. Otherwise, they will feel pressured, and no good experience will come from that for anyone.

The one thing I've learned in many years of experience when selecting the properties to show is that if the buyers are just starting their search, they might see the perfect home for them on their first visit, but since their brain is not ready, or not "tired" enough yet from seeing houses, they might miss it. It has happened so many times.

One year, I met an amazing young couple who were looking for their first home in Canada. After our initial meeting, I got their requirements, which were clearly laid down, and I'd booked some condos that were mostly matching their criteria for us to see the next day.

At that time, the market was very hot and most of the properties were selling with multiple offers and most offers were firm, without conditions. Sure enough, the first condo I showed them was a perfect match and they loved it. I looked at the listing sheet and told them I just have a favour to ask of them. They looked puzzled and asked me "What would that be?" "Forget that you ever saw this listing" I said. They looked at each other and asked: "Why?"

That unit was vacant and they were taking offers that day! I explained to them the process of placing an offer in multiple-offer situations, all the risks to it, and told them that even though it was a perfect unit for them, it was OK for them not to proceed with an offer. However, I told them that they really need to try hard not to use this listing as a comparison in the future, and not to say, "I wish we'd bought that condo." It was simply not their time, and I didn't want them to have that sadness and regret for not bidding on it. Can you imagine if they did? The first unit they saw, they bought? They would second guess that decision the very next day and would very likely doubt that decision for the rest of their lives.

We looked at quite a few listings after that one, before they finally bought a condo they liked. Did they mention the "one that got away" again? Absolutely! Almost every time we went out, but, that was OK too. It was an educated decision they made and they didn't regret it.

What I've learned from this situation is to make sure to read the FULL listing description before booking the showings. Do not create those unpleasant situations, if not needed. If I had seen that the sellers were taking offers that day, I wouldn't have shown the unit to my clients, so it would have saved some of the adrenalin rush on my clients' side. But on the other hand, they might not have seen how transparent and NOT pushy I am, and maybe they wouldn't have sent me all those leads since then? Anyway, don't overthink it! Who knows? My point is, make sure you have all the information before showing the properties. Be knowledgeable and be ready.

Here are some more showing tips for the buyers' agents that will help you as an agent along the way:

TIP 1:

☺ ALWAYS count in extra time for traffic trouble or for your clients being late when booking showings. If you run late for your first appointment, you will be late for the rest of them that day too and might run out of your scheduled showing time.

TIP 2:

☺ ALWAYS call if canceling or late. It is heartbreaking how agents disregard this line in all confirmation emails and texts they receive even if they are all in capital letters and bolded too. What is wrong with people?

They do not care if sellers had to clean the house again, after their young children just made a mess of it, or if they had to take an ill family member out of the house, so the buyer and their agent can have an empty house for them to review. Or, if they were sitting in a car eating a sandwich after a long day at work, since the buyers booked it at 6 p.m.

And, after all that hard work, no one shows up?! How would you feel if that were your mother, your sister or your spouse who was doing all that work and got stood up? Not cool, people, not cool!

PLEASE cancel your showings if you can't make it. You never know how this can pay out along the way.

Some time ago, I was showing a client a house and we went there a few times, since my client was trying to figure out a potential addition to the house. A few times we were about to be late, due to accidents on the highway, and if you live in the GTA or any other megacity, you know you absolutely can't predict the traffic flow. I made sure to call the agent each time, and ask to inform the seller about our timing, and to make sure that they would still be OK for us to go there.

After all that work and all those visits, we found out that the house would not be a good fit for my client, due to the very expensive work needed, so we moved on. That house wasn't sold and they took it off the market soon after.

A few weeks later, I received a long text message from the seller. She acknowledged my professionalism and commented that she and her husband were not satisfied with their listing agent's work and promises they made, and asked if it would be OK for her to contact me sometime in the future, for me to list their house up for sale. How is that for a payout, for doing your job, the way it should be done?

OFFER NEGOTIATION

How is your ego today?

You've spent some time showing them properties, you found them a great home and then you did your homework. You've researched the neighbourhood, schools' rankings, socio-economic and demographics report and now it's time for an offer presentation.

Before you go out for it, make sure that when you are

getting ready and changing your clothes, you leave your "Ego shirt" at home. This "getting ready" process for an offer presentation applies to you when you are getting ready to be on the sellers' side too. I'll repeat, leave the "ego-shirt" at home.

What is an "ego shirt" you ask? That is a green monster fluorescent T-shirt, that wants to flash the world on how better you are than everyone else. That little, or big, "jerk" is not supposed to be at the negotiation table. There is room for buyers, sellers and their professionally dressed agents only.

By the offer presentation time, your buyers had likely already told you what their ceiling is for that property, in regard to the purchase price and other terms. And if you are on the seller's side, likely you know what their desired outcome is too.

And, please, don't tell me you don't know it.

Even if they didn't say the specific number, which I doubt, you should have figured it out by now, by reading between the lines.

Speak with your clients. Ask questions.
⊚ What would be the best scenario for you?
⊚ What would be the worst scenario for you?
⊚ What can you live without?
⊚ What is the most definite thing you need to have in your offer?

Write all those answers down and when negotiation starts, you keep that information in front of you, in case your clients start drifting apart due to their own little "ego jerk shirt."

There was a client who got too stubborn over a very small

matter and they lost the house we were negotiating on and were never able to buy anything after that, since the market had changed and they couldn't qualify to buy anymore.

So, let's assume you know the numbers. You negotiate back and forth and both sides reach a number they can live with. This is a win-win situation, and this is unfortunately when many agents (I was one of them of course too, but now I know better) let that little "ego jerk" kick in, and try to knock that price down more, or bring the price up more, so they can show their clients how great they are.

I am not saying you shouldn't try it, (I still do it, but veeeeery carefully). But be extremely careful and read the crowd! Stop when your clients tell you they are OK with the outcome. Don't risk the other side leaving the negotiating table. It can happen.

Every time you sign back that offer, the other side has the right to accept, counter, or completely back off the deal. Your clients appreciated that you've got them the price they were expecting already. But if you lose a deal for them, they will not like you very much anymore, will they?

Your job, as their representative, is to create a rapport with the other agent, and together to build a golden bridge between the buyers and sellers, and let THEM meet their minds, and wrap it nicely with a "win-win" bow.

Sellers will be happy, Buyers will be happy, both agents will be happy, and we shouldn't be worrying too much about that little "ego jerk." Let him go and ruin someone else's life.

BE A FRIEND NOT A FOE
(READ "JERK")

When dealing with an agent on the other side of the table, you should show respect and treat them equally, regardless of the market you are in, experience level, brand or anything else.

So many times we were feeling dismissed by the listing agents when the market was hot, and from the buyers' agents when the market was down. Sometimes, we simply had to deal with agents who have huge egos and no professionalism at all, regardless of which side of the table they are.

Many years ago, a client of mine decided to place an offer on a property that was backing onto train tracks. That listing was on the market for a very long time, even though the market was good, so my client decided to lowball it. We went in with a low initial offer, with intention to increase it. I went to the house, so I could present it in person. The listing agent saw the offer and went bonkers. She screamed, and was shooting insults at me for some time, in rapid fire! I listened patiently, without responding back to her mean words, thanked them for the opportunity for me to present my client's offer and left. We had decided not to improve our offer that night and left home. Three days later my phone rang. It was the same agent: "Hi honey," she said. I removed my phone from my ear to look if that was really her name on the phone display. Yup, it was her. "How can I help you?" I asked. "Well, we are hoping that you will come back with another offer since my client wants to sell," she said. I told her that I would speak with my client and get back to her. We went back with an EVEN LOWER offer then the first time, and we GOT IT!

Had she kept her cool the first time, her clients would have gotten more money, and her clients would appreciate her work way more than the outcome that happened.

Some (read many) agents forget that they are NOT the stars of the show, but that they are at the negotiation table to HELP their clients meet minds.

When the market is on your side, just because you think you have an upper hand at the negotiation table at the moment, that doesn't mean you have to treat the other side as less worthy.

I find that is one of the major mistakes agents make. They somehow forget that the table turns and you will likely be sitting on the other side soon. So, next time you receive an offer on your listing, or you are submitting an offer, please be courteous, acknowledge the other agent and their hard work, and try to work TOGETHER on building that golden bridge we were talking about earlier. Believe me, it can be really pleasant working like that. The whole real estate transaction goes smoothly, and you gain a new friend, so next time they are sitting on the other side of the table, you know that you are in for a great transaction. I've had the privilege of working with quite a few great agents like that, but still not nearly enough.

Many agents still live in a "scarcity" mentality, which doesn't do good to anyone. Which one are you?

CHAPTER 11

BE A "ONE STOP SHOP" FOR YOUR CLIENTS

I believe that one of the pillars for a successful real estate business is your relationship with your past clients. According to a National Association of Realtors (U.S.) survey from 2018, only 12 per cent of homebuyers and sellers have used the same agent they've used before. Why do you think that is? Agents tend to forget their clients within a few years, unless they have a great client-management system in place. Now, this is actually good news for you, since you can scoop up those 88 per cent of clients by your great work and your great connection with your past clients, who will then refer those 88 per cent to you ☺

How will you do this? Once you firm up a deal, make sure your clients know you have a database of trustworthy service providers and they can reach out to you anytime, if they themselves or anyone they know needs any kind of those services. If they need a great accountant, make sure you have three of those. If they ask for a good plumber, make sure you have some of them too. Even if they ask you for a great dentist, you should have an amazing one in your database too.

You see how I didn't say "ask if they need a realtor"? By sending your trusted other services, whose name will they constantly mention? Yours, of course. This is another way of "soft selling," which will likely get you faster and more qualified referrals, as opposed to if you keep reminding them you are a realtor and asking their friends and neighbours if they want to buy or sell real estate.

Make sure you write down all those great lawyers you've dealt with, those contractors, mortgage brokers, doctors, day cares and more. As a matter of fact, be so resourceful that your clients will put your name on a speed dial. (Man, I'm old! I meant to put your name in "favourites.") Why? Because if they see your name daily, how likely do you think they will refer you next time someone is asking for a good real estate agent, or are complaining about their current one and think all agents are like that? Your clients will become your advocates who will point out that you are way better, and you always go above and beyond for your clients.

You are probably asking yourself, where can you find those services? Do not worry, even if you just landed in this country yesterday, you could do it! Start by asking your colleagues and friends who do they know and trust and start your own database by adding those services. With social media platforms and professional group pages, you can start there too, to collect names and services.

Your question should be something like:
- ◎ "Which services you have used recently and were so happy with them that you would be using their services again, and would highly recommend them to others?"

As you start trading more, you will keep meeting new people and services. Your referral book should never be "full," but should be constantly growing. Become your clients', friends' and family's' "Trusted Yellow Pages." For the "new kids on the block," that means become their "Trusted Google Search Engine."

CONCLUSION

In our market area (the GTA) there are over 73,000 real estate agents registered in 2023, and we have a joke saying that if you throw a rock at a group of people, it is likely you will hit at least four real estate agents with one rock.

Having said that, you really need to stand out, so the clients can pick you, whether your market is just a fraction of ours, or if it is much bigger than ours too.

Why not do it by your great knowledge, work ethic and honorable reputation?

Have you noticed that I didn't mention experience?

Even though experience is important in our business, if you follow most of the tips and ideas I've provided you in this book, and with some help from your office and more experienced colleagues who are willing to help you, of course, I am sure you will thrive in this business.

If you follow the roadmap I've showed you in this book, and you use and follow all the tips on how to select and connect with your future clients, how to understand and pre-qualify your clients, and how to "breeze" through a real estate transaction, I am sure that going through your first year in real estate will be a remarkable one, and you will keep building on your success! Don't worry if the market is at its lowest or at its highest. Focus on your tasks, surround yourself with positive and successful people. As the amazing Les Brown says: "OQP" – ONLY QUALIFIED PEOPLE. Tune out the negativity from everyday news and you will be OK.

Do good, be good and more good will come your way. Be respectful toward your clients and colleagues and people will notice that. Trust me.

I sincerely hope that this book will help you build a foundation of your successful real estate business and that you will keep rising, as high as you don't even dare to imagine at this moment! However, please remember that this book is simply a tool, here to help you along the way, and you will still need to do the work! Think of yourself as a curious three-year-old and keep asking questions. Keep using those amazing Where, When, What and Why and you will be just fine.

If you liked this book and you are curious to learn more, feel free to connect with me at:

Results@MatildaHomes.ca

And if this book helped you, i would REALLY love to know. Please share your success story with me at:
www.StopSellingRealEstate.com

ABOUT THE AUTHOR

Matilda Nestoroska is an award-winning real estate broker with almost two decades of experience on two continents. Her knowledge, experience, love and respect for the industry made her always willing to help and educate the public and mentor new agents. Matilda is a respected member of the TRREB, Oakville and Milton real estate boards and a member of CREA, OREA, NAR and REBAC. Throughout the years, she has achieved quite a few designations, including Certified Negotiating Expert (CNE), Accredit Buyers Representative (ABR) and Member of Institute for Luxury Home Marketing (MILHM). Matilda is a recipient of many awards, including RE/MAX's Hall of Fame award, #3 Agent for RE/MAX Aboutowne Realty Head office for 2022, and is a longtime member of Business Network International (BNI).

INDENT PUBLISHING BOOKS

Books by author David W. Barber
with illustrations by Dave Donald

A Musician's Dictionary
(1983)
(Revised and expanded in 2011 as
Accidentals on Purpose: A Musician's Dictionary)

Bach, Beethoven and the Boys:
Music History as It Ought to Be Taught
(1986, 35th-anniversary edition revised 2021)

Bach, Beethoven Going Baroque:
Even More Music History as It Ought to Be Taught
(2023)

Bach, Beethoven and the Grrrls
Women's Music History As It Ought To Be Taught
(2024)

When the Fat Lady Sings:
Opera History as It Ought to Be Taught
(1990)

If It Ain't Baroque:
More Music History as It Ought to Be Taught
(1992, 30th-anniversary edition revised 2022)

Getting a Handel on Messiah
(1995, 30th-anniversary edition revised 2025)

Tutus, Tights and Tiptoes:
Ballet History as It Ought to Be Taught
(2000, revised edition 2023)

Other Books by David W. Barber

The Last Laugh:
Essays and Oddities in the News
(2000)

Quotable Alice
(2001)

Quotable Sherlock
(2001)

Quotable Twain
(2002)

The Adventure of the Sunken Parsley:
and Other Stories of Sherlock Holmes
(2011)

Better Than it Sounds:
The Music Lover's Quotation Book
(2013)

Think Again!
by Leo Tolstoy, with annotations and commentary
by David W. Barber
(2022)

Atonement and other stories
(2022)

Leacock Laughter
(2023)

Hedshot
(2023)

Mugshot
(2024)

Other Books by Indent Publishing

Learn to Play
Susie Beghin
(2022)

Parents Learn to Play Too
Susie Beghin
(2024)

A Feast of Wolves
Wilson Coneybeare
(2023)

Wild Strawberries Along the Mackenzie
Bernard R. Blishen
(2023)

Find all Indent books at our website:
IndentPublishing.com

www.ingramcontent.com/pod-product-compliance
Lightning Source LLC
Chambersburg PA
CBHW071837200326
41519CB00016B/4139